ZEN WAY—JESUS WAY

Tucker N. Callaway

ZEN WAY

JESUS WAY

CHARLES E. TUTTLE COMPANY
Rutland · Vermont : Tokyo · Japan

Published by the Charles E. Tuttle Company, Inc.
of Rutland, Vermont & Tokyo, Japan
with editorial offices at
Suido 1-chome, 2-6 Bunkyo-ku, Tokyo 112

LCC Card No. 76-6032
ISBN 0-8048-1885-1

First edition, 1976
First paperback edition, 1992

Printed in Japan

To

DAISETZ T. SUZUKI

teacher and friend

TABLE OF CONTENTS

FOREWORD

by Masatoshi Doi
Director, NCC Center for the Study of Japanese Religions

IT IS A great honor for me to write a foreword to this book by Dr. Tucker Callaway, an old friend of mine. As far as I know, few Protestant missionaries have immersed themselves as deeply as Dr. Callaway in the study and experience of Buddhism, especially Zen. As he testifies in this book, his second on Buddhism, Dr. Callaway succeeded in reaching the state of mind which Zen calls Enlightenment.

In 1966 the NCC Center for the Study of Japanese Religions sponsored a seminar on Zen for Japanese pastors and invited three Zen masters as lecturers. After a lengthy discussion using such ontological terms as Being, Nonbeing, Nothingness, Absolute Nothingness, and Emptiness, I put this question to a relatively young Zen master who had studied under Martin Heidegger: "Which do you prefer to call Zen, an ontology or a way of life (*Lebensweisheit*)?" His immediate answer was, "*Lebensweisheit!*" This sufficiently justifies the title of this book: *Zen Way—Jesus Way*, the juxtaposition of the two ways. After all, all religions are different ways of life in different social and historical contexts. Their metaphysical expressions are later products of reflection.

"No dependence upon the words and letters of the scriptures!" (*furyū monji* in Japanese). This is the first principle of Zen. And yet, paradoxically enough, Zen scholars speak and write more than any other Buddhist scholars. Those who hear them and read their books tend to think, "Now I understand Zen. It's interesting, isn't it." But they are deluded. To know what Zen really means, Dr. Callaway was wise to supplement his reading with personal contacts and finally to undergo long, painstaking training.

In the 33rd vow of the Larger Sukhāvatī-vyuha (*Daimuryōjūkyō* in Japanese) it is promised that all who bask in the eternal light of Amidha Buddha will have their minds and bodies softened and made flexible like those of the multitudes in heaven. In Matthew 4 : 4 it is said, "Blessed are the meek, for they shall inherit the earth." In both Buddhism and Christianity, meekness or soft-mindedness is one of the basic features of the blessed ones. Dr. Callaway's soft-mindedness and flexibility enabled him, I am sure, to penetrate deep into the hearts of such great Zen personalities as those mentioned in Section II and into their wisdom as related in Section I. In these sections he synthesizes the Mādhyamika and Yogācāra schools, the two main streams of Mahayana Buddhism, though his emphasis falls on the latter.

In Section III Dr. Callaway presents a comparative study of the Zen Way and the Jesus Way. It is rather natural that he, being a Protestant theologian, finds more dividing points than converging points in the two ways of life. The reader should compare Dr. Callaway's approach with those of Catholic scholars such as Heinrich Dumoulin (*Christianity Meets Buddhism*) and H. M. Enomiya Lassalle (*Zen Meditation for Christians*). They are better equipped in their approach to Zen due to the contribution of Catholic mystics in the Middle Ages and to the traditional doctrine of *logos spermatikos* (the seminal Logos, or seed of reason, by which Christ is dimly perceived apart from his revelation in the person of Jesus—a doctrine used by Catholic scholars to account for features common to Christianity and other religions and philosophies). But points that divide the Zen Way from the Jesus Way are unavoidable for one who is faithful to the Protestant principle of *sola gratia* (by grace alone), which stresses the historical revelation of Jesus and thus denies any human role in salvation.

With this new book Dr. Callaway, as a Protestant, has made a fresh contribution to this important area of interfaith dialogue between Zen and Christianity. His literary skill has made this book easily understandable and enjoyable for both specialists and lay readers.

National Christian Council Center
Kyoto

PREFACE

I WOULD NOT have written this book if I had ever seen another one like it. I believe it is unique. For some thirty years I have been both a committed Christian and a dedicated student of Buddhism. My chief interest in graduate research was the philosophy of the world's major religions. My doctoral dissertation on the concept of deliverance in Buddhism of the Mahayana type, published under the title *Japanese Buddhism and Christianity*, was the result not only of considerable reading in the field but also of countless hours of firsthand experience in the major Buddhist temples of Japan.

My assignment as a Christian missionary for about twenty years in that country was to teach World Religions and Philosophy of Religion at Seinan Gakuin University in the city of Fukuoka. As I shall indicate in the pages which follow, I had both the incentive and the opportunity to gain access to the heart of the faith of earnest Buddhist adherents not granted to many Westerners. Section II of this book is an account of some of my personal contacts with Buddhist priests and teachers, including the widely beloved Dr. Daisetz T. Suzuki. My debt to such men will become apparent. My gratitude to them is profound.

This book is intended for anyone with an interest in the subject suggested by the title. Even if the reader has known little of the Zen Way before, or even if he has known little of the Jesus Way before, I believe I have written in a style which is not too technical to be interesting and informative.

On the other hand, this book is especially for Buddhist monks, priests, teachers, and sincere lay followers of the Zen Way. It is also for Christian theologians, pastors, missionaries, and all who have chosen to walk the Jesus Way. In Charles Williams's delicious novel *War in Heaven*, Mr. Mornington, the publisher, commented to the Archdeacon concerning his newly submitted manuscript, "I gather that this is at once specialist and popular."[1] I dare hope my own offering is the same.

It is in three sections: the first is a presentation of the fundamental presuppositions of Zen and several of the concepts which are logically deduced from them; the second is an account of interviews with Buddhist monks and teachers met in major temples, chiefly in Kyoto, in which I try to show how the concepts introduced in Section One are practically applied; the third is an attempt to state the fundamentals of the Jesus Way in a manner which permits meaningful comparison with the fundamentals of the Zen Way.

Over the years I have done considerable reading of Bud-

[1]Charles Williams, *War in Heaven* (London: Faber & Faber Ltd., 1947), pp. 22f.

dhist sutras and related writings in Chinese and Japanese ideographs. Most of the translations in the book are my own. In several cases I have given the ideographs or their Japanese pronunciation in parallel with their English meaning in such a way that one who knows no Chinese or Japanese can get a feel of the original and make his own translation.

When pronunciation is given in Roman letters, it is the Japanese, not the Chinese. A few simple rules concerning Japanese vowel sounds will, I believe, be helpful. Each vowel has only one sound, as follows:

"a" as in *father*
"e" as in *help*
"i" as in *meet*, *machine*
"o" as in *hold*
"u" as in *blue*

There is one definitive change for vowels, not in sound or tone, but in length. The short vowel is cut abruptly; the long vowel is lengthened noticeably. I have indicated the difference by placing a macron over the vowel when it is long; otherwise, it is short. For example, the word for Middle-Way is Chū-dō. It is pronounced "chew-dough," but both the "u" and the "o" sound should be slightly prolonged. The length of the vowel is important in signifying meaning: for instance, *ku* means suffering; *kū* means emptiness.

In general, to save the reader the need to learn many new words, I have used capitalized English to denote the Sanskrit-Chinese-Japanese technical terms. At least the first time one of these is introduced, I give its Japanese pronunciation with it and the Chinese ideographs in a footnote at the bottom of the page. At the end of the book there is a glossary of most of the terms employed.

It is impossible to express appreciation to the hundreds of Buddhists who have aided me in my research over the years. I will thank several of them by name in the appropriate place in the book itself. In dedicating the work to Daisetz Suzuki, I am acknowledging a mammoth debt. The study of more than a dozen of his books as well as the privilege of personal interviews have been a major influence in my academic life. The last chapter of Section II consists chiefly of one of the precious conversations we had together.

I am also grateful to several colleagues who travel the Jesus Way for reading the manuscript. Their request for clarification at various points in what was for them a novel field led to revisions which I believe will be a help to others for whom Zen is new. Many thanks to Pat Bellinger for typing my messy manuscript, and especially to F. Calvin Parker of the Japan Baptist Mission for his painstaking editing.

And I am pleased to thank my long-time friend, Masatoshi Doi, Professor of Systematic Theology at Doshisha University and Director of the NCC Center for the Study of Japanese Religions in Kyoto, for his many kindnesses over the years. Much of my reading was done in the facilities of his Center. Some of my most rewarding Buddhist contacts were made through his introduction. I further thank him for supplying the Foreword to this book.

—Tucker N. Callaway

ACKNOWLEDGMENTS

GRATEFUL acknowledgments are made to the following for permissions to quote from copyrighted materials:

John Weatherhill, Inc., Tokyo, for *The Three Pillars of Zen: Teaching, Practice, and Enlightenment*, compiled and edited by Philip Kapleau, Copyright 1965 by Philip Kapleau.

Mrs. Laura Huxley and Chatto & Windus Ltd., London; and Harper & Row, Publishers, Inc., New York, for *Brave New World* by Aldous Huxley (Penguin Modern Classics, 1955), Copyright the Estate of Aldous Huxley 1932.

Daito Shuppansha, Tokyo, for *Japanese-English Buddhist Dictionary* (1965).

Charles E. Tuttle Co., Inc., Tokyo, for *A Flower Does Not Talk: Zen Essays* by Zenkei Shibayama, translated by Sumiko Kudo (1970).

Matsugaoka Bunko, Kamakura (Shokin Furuta, Dir tor) for the D. T. Suzuki–T. N. Callaway interview published in *The Eastern Buddhist*, New Series, Vol No. 1 (June 1970).

Bible quotations followed by "RSV" are taken from the Revised Standard Version, copyright 1946 and 1952 by the Division of Christian Education of the National Council of the Churches of Christ in the United States of America; those followed by "TEV" are taken from the New Testament in Today's English Version, copyright 1966 by the American Bible Society. Other Bible quotations are the author's own renderings.

SECTION

I

THE LOGIC OF ZEN

When Starting from Its Own Presuppositions: The Mind Is Everything and Everything Is Nothing

1

IT WAS twilight as I wandered through the spacious grounds of Nanzen-ji[1] in the ancient city of Kyoto. Overhead the rush of water through the brick trough of the ivy-covered aqueduct mingled with wind sighs from boughs of gigantic pines. Tasting the fragrance of burning needles, I moved toward the red glow of a tiny fire deep in tree shadows. A black-robed monk was at his task of raking clean the sand. After timeless moments of pregnant silence, I spoke:

"What is your intention in Zen?"

"To be this smoke!" he replied.

All had been said.

Zen Buddhism is a revolutionary way of experiencing the world and oneself. Its consequence is radical and complete deliverance from suffering. Its life-style is epitomized in two apparently contradictory poems from the distant past.

Bamboo shadows sweep
stairs of stone,
But the dust on them
stirs not.[2]

[1]Nanzen-ji: J., *-ji* 寺; literally, "temple." Instead of Nanzen Temple, I am using the Japanese form of the temple's name. I will do the same for temple names throughout the book.

[2]竹影掃堦塵不動

The other:

> Divine way,
> Awesome activity:
> To draw water!
> To carry firewood![3]

The first poem suggests detachment. Although the shadows move, nothing moves. And this motionless movement moves nothing. The dust on those moon-flecked stairs is not swept by the sweeping shadows. There is no effect, for there is no cause.

If the first depicts detachment, the second poem indicates involvement. Even such simple tasks as drawing water from a well or carrying an armload of firewood from a forest are performed with an intensity of awareness which causes it to take on a mystical aura akin to holy ritual.

Complete detachment, total involvement—both at the same time! These are the twin characteristics of the Zen Way.

How can such diametrically opposite attitudes reign whole and reconciled within a single heart without a schizoid rending? Is it not mere nonsense to propose that the simultaneous experiencing of two such mutually exclusive responses to life can lead to peace of mind?

The answer to such questions lies in the direction of the following testimony by an ex-businessman from New York, Mr. Philip Kapleau. In an entry in his diary on April 1, 1953, he wrote: ". . . Belly aching all week, Doc says ulcers are getting worse. . . . So miserable wish I had the guts to end it all."[4] Taking a long look at what he had become, he

[3] 神通 並妙用荷水也搬柴

[4] Philip Kapleau, comp. and ed., *The Three Pillars of Zen* (Tokyo: John Weatherhill Inc., 1965), p. 208.

resolved to leave the New York rat race. Forthwith he went to Japan, took up residence in a series of Zen temples under a series of Zen masters, spent countless hours doing Za-zen[5] while concentrating on various Kōan.[6] At last, on August 5, 1958, he found what he had been seeking. Hear him describe the culminating moments of his Quest:

> Threw myself into Mu [No-thing-ness][7] for another nine hours with such utter absorption that *I* completely vanished. . . . *I* didn't eat breakfast, *Mu* did. *I* didn't sweep and wash the floors after breakfast, *Mu* did. . . . Afternoon dokusan![8] . . . Hawklike, the roshi[9] scrutinized me as I entered his room, walked toward him, prostrated myself, and sat before him with my mind alert and exhilarated. . . .
> "The universe is One," he began, each word tearing into my mind like a bullet. "The moon of Truth—" All at once the roshi, the room, every single thing disappeared in a dazzling stream of illumination and I felt myself bathed in a delicious, unspeakable delight. . . . For a fleeting eternity I was alone—I alone was. . . . Then the roshi swam into view. Our eyes met and flowed into each other, and we burst out laughing. . . . "I have it! I know! There is nothing, absolutely nothing. I am everything and everything is nothing!" I exclaimed

[5]J., Za-zen 坐禪; literally, "seated-meditation."

[6]J., Kō-an 公案; literally, "public-notice." These Zen anecdotes and their use will be explained more fully in later chapters.

[7]J., Mu 無; used in Buddhism to designate No-thing-ness, No-thing, the non-objectivity of things. In general usage it can mean simple negation (no) or denial of existence (not, or nothing).

[8]J., Doku-san 獨參; literally, "alone-visit." Private visit of a seeker with his master.

[9]J., Rō-shi 老師; literally, "aged-teacher." A Zen master.

more to myself than to the roshi, and got up and walked out. . . .[10]

With this exclamation, the ex-businessman from New York gave evidence he had experienced the Zen Realization designated by such Japanese terms as Satori,[11] Kenshō,[12] and Bodai.[13] Although he had verbalized the substance of his experience in a more abstract and intellectual form than is usually allowed, the spontaneity of that verbalization attested to its authenticity. More often such a breakthrough is affirmed by some wordless gesture or apparently unrelated comment.

Be that as it may, the very intellectuality of Kapleau's ejaculation is helpful. "There is nothing, absolutely nothing. I am everything and everything is nothing!" Here is a simple, lucid statement of how a Zen-man sees himself and the world. And it is this point of view which allows him the tranquility of simultaneous detachment and involvement which is the hallmark of Zen deliverance.

It is customary to call the paradoxes so prevalent in Zen teachings alogical or even irrational. When a Rōshi asks us to hear the clap-sound of a single hand or to detect the scent of the color blue, we Westerners are apt to say he's talking nonsense. If we start with our materialistic, pluralistic presuppositions, we must judge them so. What I want to show in the ensuing pages is that once the presuppositions of the Zen view of reality are firmly grasped, all the strange affirmations and antics of the Zen masters are logically consistent and

[10]Kapleau, *Three Pillars*, pp. 227f.

[11]J., Satori 悟; literally, "realization."

[12]J., Ken-shō 見性; literally, "see-reality."

[13]J., Bo-dai 菩提; transliteration of Skt., Bodhi, meaning to awaken from sleep and, by extension, to awaken to the truth.

thoroughly reasonable. On Zen premises, complete detachment and total involvement—both at once—are just what reason would lead us to expect. On those premises, Kapleau's exclamation, "I am everything and everything is nothing!" is a plain statement of fact.

I take this approach with apologies to the many Zen friends who have sought to assist me in my search for an understanding of their position. I believe they will agree with the substance of what I am about to say. They will not, however, care much for my emphasis upon the rationality of Zen—not because it is untrue, but because they know one can never come at the Zen experience itself through reason.

They will, I think, be in accord with a major objective of this book: to expose the foolishness written about Zen by some Western authors who have dabbled in it enough to learn some of its techniques and terminology, but have missed its essence. These undertake the meaningless task of trying to graft Zen-isms upon the body of their Occidental habits of thought. I have heard Zen masters laugh at the absurdities which result. To beloved Buddhist teachers in Japan like Daisetz Suzuki, Zenkei Shibayama, Sohaku Ogata, Saizo Inagaki, and many others who gave of their profound understanding to help me, I pledge my earnest intention to present the Zen Buddhist position with complete faithfulness. If anything, this intention is strengthened by the fact that some of them have since passed away.

My apologies to them for stating in what I hope will be a clear, rational form what they would prefer to remain on the level of provocative encounter and abstruse comment. It is not that they wish to obscure what they believe to be the truth. Their reluctance to say it as plainly as I am about to do derives from their knowledge that the experiential insight of Satori is often more difficult to achieve if the seeker begins by acquiring merely an ideational grasp of basic precepts. It is easy for him to confuse his abstract understanding with true Realization. A chemist who has successfully analyzed the organic structure of sugar molecules does not thereby discover its flavor. He can only taste its sweetness by putting some on his tongue.

While my Zen friends will agree that if one starts from Zen assumptions the possibility of hearing the clap of only one hand is wholly logical, they will shake their heads and sigh, "Yes. But understanding the logic of it is not hearing the sound of the clap!"

They will be correct.

Having conceded this, I venture to believe that rational explanation will at least have the negative value of preventing mistaken notions of what Zen is. Reading what I will have to say may not put the taste of sugar on the tongue, but it should prevent confusing the substance of sugar with the substance of salt. It may even help the seeker to know in which direction the sugar is to be found.

• 2 •

"THERE IS nothing! Absolutely nothing! I am everything and everything is nothing!" From the standpoint of Western materialistic pluralism this is an utterly incomprehensible statement; from the standpoint of Zen it is a perfectly logical and straightforward affirmation of the facts of existence. The key word is "nothing," or more clearly, "no-thing." The Japanese is Mu.

One of the most familiar Kōan is the first anecdote in the *Mu-mon Kan* (No-Gate Gateway) known as "Jōshū's Dog":

> A monk once asked Jōshū, "Has a dog the Buddha-Nature?"
> Jōshū replied, "Mu!"[1]

Mu can be taken as a simple negation, "No," as if Jōshū were saying a dog does not have the Buddha-Nature. This misses the point altogether. Here, and in Zen generally, Mu means No-thing. A dog is not a thing; the Buddha-Nature is not a thing. This is the significance of Jōshū's reply, "Mu!"

You will remember that the morning before his Kenshō, Kapleau was focusing his attention on Mu; not so much on the word, but on the nature of reality it implies. Hear him once more. This time I will translate Mu where it occurs:

> Threw myself into No-thing for another nine hours with such utter absorption that *I* completely vanished. . . . *I* didn't eat breakfast, *No-thing* did. *I* didn't sweep and wash the floors after breakfast, *No-thing* did.[2]

His Kenshō ejaculation is not merely a reiteration of the word, but evidence of going behind it to the experience of the reality to which it points: "There is No-thing! Absolutely No-thing! . . . Everything is No-thing!"

Clearly he had come to the same view of things as denoted by Jōshū's "Mu!" In the same way that there was no dog which might attain the Buddha-Nature and no Buddha-Nature to be obtained, so there was no individual who ate

[1]Among various English translations of the *Mu-Mon Kan* is one which also includes the original Chinese: R. H. Blyth, *Zen and Zen Classics*, Volume Four, *Mumonkan* (Tokyo: Hokuseido Press, 1966); the First Anecdote is on page 22.

[2]Kapleau, *Three Pillars*, p. 227.

breakfast and washed floors, or any breakfast to be eaten, or floors to be washed.

There is absolutely No-thing! No particular three-dimensional objects in three-dimensional space exist, have ever existed, will ever exist! There are no acting, knowing, feeling selves; there is no material environment composed of such entities as mountains and elephants and hickory nuts. Every-thing is No-thing! This is one fundamental presupposition of Zen.

The other is, "I am everything!" Just before this utterance, Kapleau had said:

> All at once the roshi, the room, every single thing disappeared in a dazzling stream of illumination and I felt myself bathed in a delicious, unspeakable delight. . . . For a fleeting eternity I was alone—I alone was.[3]

There is nothing but an "I" who is everything. This "I" is not the separate, individual person named Kapleau who had been a businessman in New York and was now seated in a temple room facing another individual person, his Rōshi. This "I" is rather the mind in whose consciousness everything has its existence. No-thing eats breakfast, washes floors, visits a Rōshi. The empirical self with a face and a body identified by a particular name is merely one of the thought-images in that consciousness. A living body, like everything else, is No-thing.

"I was alone." When the mind in whose consciousness everything appears is emptied of all images, it experiences

[3]Ibid., p. 228. Having acknowledged that the particular verbal statement of these two propositions is Kapleau's, I will use them with flexibility as to wording henceforth, and usually without quotation marks.

itself alone: an undifferentiated screen of pure awareness. "I alone was." Mind in this state of undifferentiated awareness perceives that it itself is the only existence.

Before this Enlightenment experience, the mind is deceived in distinguishing between itself and the ideational creations of its own imagination. Doubtless you, the reader, think that your mind is inside your head looking out through your eyes to see the pages of this book now held in your hand as you sit in a chair in a room somewhere. If so—according to Zen—you are totally deceived.

With Kenshō, you would realize that your head, your eyes, the book, the chair, the room, everything you can see out the window, all you are thinking and feeling about these things—absolutely everything you are now experiencing is completely a fabrication of your consciousness. Only your mind exists. There is No-thing outside your mind; there has never been anything outside your mind; there will never be anything outside your mind. Your mind is everything. You can say, "I am everything! Everything is No-thing!"

After a long habit of believing that the people, the places, the things you know through your five senses are external to and independent of your mind, it seems an intolerable enormity to move to the opposite position. This is the stumbling block, the monstrous revolution of understanding which your mind resists with agonizing desperation. To believe it would be to unmake and remake the world.

The thing to be believed is quite simple: there is nothing outside your mind. It is not difficult to understand this proposition with your intellect. The problem is to believe it is actually true—to believe to the extent that you will live as if it were true. I have said Zen is not words, but an experience. The heart of the matter is to *experience* your life in the world as if you are everything and everything is No-thing.

If you should do so you would find, on the one hand, that nothing is changed. You would continue meeting the same people, seeing the same face in the mirror, tasting the same food, thinking the same thoughts, having the same emotions as before. On the other hand, you would find everything changed. Realizing that No-thing is, you would accept everything which happens with detachment. Since everything is your mind's dream, you would observe it all with such an intensity of interest you would be totally involved in it. It is this experience of complete detachment and total involvement—both at the same time—which I have said is the distinguishing characteristic of the Zen life-style.

If you lived that way, you would smile just as Jōshū at the naiveté of the question, "Does a dog have the Buddha-Nature?" You would know that a dog is not a thing and the Buddha-Nature is not a thing and, therefore, that the question presupposes a kind of world which does not exist. To such a question you would quite logically give the same sort of exasperated reply, "No-thing!"

"I am everything and everything is No-thing!"—not these specific words, but the position they indicate—is like the "da-da-da-daaah" of Beethoven's Fifth Symphony. The various terms, anecdotes, illustrations, and techniques given in Zen literature and practice are like the interwoven repetitions of that major theme in differing tempo, key, and volume which constitute the body of the symphony.

The remainder of this book must be repetitive in the same way. The major theme will be expressed in several of the different forms utilized by Zen itself.

• 3 •

WHAT FOLLOWS in the remainder of Section I and also in Section II will simply confirm and clarify the position set forth in the previous chapter. I will now begin a review of some of the terms traditionally used by Buddhists to present their point of view.

Zen says your mind alone exists. Everything of which you are conscious through your senses, all your reasoning, your emotions are, like dreams, completely nonspatial, nonpluralistic, nonmaterial, and "subjective." There are several technical terms which designate the all-embracing Mind which is, in fact, "your" mind. Some of these are: Buddha-Mind (Bus-shin),[1] Only-Mind (Yui-shin),[2] One-Mind (Is-shin),[3] and No-thing-Mind (Mu-shin).[4] This Mind is sometimes, although less frequently, referred to as the Self; for example, Only-Self (Yui-ga)[5] and No-thing-Self (Mu-ga).[6]

For the sake of clarity, I wish to distinguish between the Zen view of Mind and that of most Western idealistic philosophies. Immanuel Kant teaches that a man can only know the contents of his own consciousness, Phenomena, but can never know the things in the world external to his consciousness as they actually are in themselves, Noumena. The structure of the eyes, ears, and other sense organs, the structure

[1]Buddha-Mind: J., Bus-shin 佛心; literal translation as also in notes 2–9.

[2]Only-Mind; J., Yui-shin 唯心.

[3]One-Mind: J., Is-shin 一心.

[4]No-thing-Mind; J., Mu-shin 無心.

[5]Only-Self: J., Yui-ga 唯我.

[6]No-thing-Self: J., Mu-ga 無我.

of the nerves which conduct the responses of these organs to the brain, and the various categories of the brain itself which transform these responses into images in the consciousness—all shape and color everything which appears in that consciousness. As I write, I see in my hand a yellow-and-black-striped ball-point pen. I understand, however, that the yellowness, blackness, hardness, and surface smoothness of the pen are qualities constructed by my own brain and nervous system. Such characteristics are part of that world of which I have immediate knowledge inside my consciousness, that is, the Phenomenal world. But what this pen is in itself in its molecular, atomic, and subatomic structure—the pen as it actually exists in the Noumenal world external to my body—is absolutely inconceivable to me. And yet I believe, and Kant believed, that things such as my pen exist in that external world, whatever they may be in themselves. Kant held that Phenomenal experience inside the mind is in response to stimuli in the Noumenal world outside the mind.

Zenists can agree with Kant that all which can be known is within the mind, but they must completely reject his view that the images in the consciousness are Phenomenal responses to some sort of world outside the mind. The very concepts "inside" and "outside" are meaningless from the standpoint of Zen.

There is Only-Mind!

One of the favorite Buddhist illustrations of Only-Mind is that of a mirror and its "reflections." To grasp the significance of this illustration it must be understood from the outset that the "reflections" are not reflections of things outside the mirror, but are generated by the mirror itself like pictures on a television screen. Looking into this magical mirror one gains the impression that the "reflections" are

three-dimensional objects moving about in three-dimensional space. If, as in a performance of theatrical magic, the mirror is placed so that its presence is not detectable, one would be convinced that its "reflections" are actual, material things. Yet one knows that in fact there is no depth dimension, no space, no substantial object, and no movement in a mirror. If I put my hand on the face of a mirror in which things seem to be moving about, I find it motionless and the "things" in it not to be touched or grasped. They may seem to be separated by great distances as, for instance, a mountain far in the background, or a broad expanse of ocean. I know this spatial extension is merely appearance, not fact.

In Satori, Only-Mind (your mind) comes to realize that everything it has ever experienced or will ever experience is like those "reflections"; Only-Mind itself is the mirror. There is Only-Mind.

Since the existing Self is that Mind, everything just said about Only-Mind (Yui-shin) can also be said about Only-Self (Yui-ga). You could reread the above substituting the word Only-Self for Only-Mind. It is for this reason the Enlightened Zenist can say, "I am everything and everything is No-thing!" Precisely! Everything which *is* is within your Mind and is identical with your Self. Apart from that Self there is No-thing. There is Only-Self. "I am alone; I alone am."

Only-Mind, Only-Self, is the Buddha-Mind (Bus-shin). It is also called the Buddha-Reality (Bus-shō).[7] Ken-shō means seeing this Reality. Although sometimes used as if it were a personal name, the word Buddha is essentially the designation of a mind-state. Its Sanskrit root, "Budh" or "Bodh" means simply to awake from sleep or to regain

[7]**Buddha-Reality: J., Bus-shō 佛性.**

consciousness. Only-Mind is both the source of its own awakening and the contents of its awakened consciousness. It is, therefore, Buddha-Mind; it is Buddha-Reality.

Even though one sees that there is Only-Mind, Only-Self, and sees that this Mind-Self is the Buddha-Mind and that it constitutes Buddha-Reality, subtle dangers to understanding yet remain. First, there may still lurk the possibility of conceiving a distinction between the Mind-Self of yourself and the Mind-Self of other selves. To prevent this, the term One-Mind (Is-shin) is used. There is no plurality of minds located in a plurality of individual ego-centers. There is Only-Mind, and this Mind is single and alone in all the universe; rather, all the universe has its being in One-Mind, single and alone. Your Mind, your consciousness, your Self only is. There is nothing else.

Western philosophy has a term, solipsism (from the Latin *sol-ipse*; literally, only self), which, from one point of view, describes the Zen position very well. In fact the base of the Japanese word for solipsism is the same Yui-ga which is found in Buddhism. (The Japanese for solipsism is Yui-ga-ron, *-ron* being the equivalent to the English -ism.) But here we come to the second threat to a proper understanding of the Zen world-view. Having found that there is Only-Mind, the Buddha-Mind, and that this Mind is One-Mind, there still remains the possibility of picturing this One-Mind as a single thing. There is No-thing. The One-Mind is not a three-dimensional brain like a football suspended in three-dimensional space. Only-Mind, the Buddha-Mind, is not a particular entity with a particular spatial location. There is no entity; there is no space. Only-Mind is the No-thing-Mind (Mu-shin); Only-Self is the No-thing-Self (Mu-ga).

The Mind-Self alone is, but it is not something with form and substance. It *is*. *What* it is is inconceivable. Any idea

it may have of itself must take some particular form, but any such concrete conception must be nothing more than another image made up in its own consciousness, not a picture corresponding to what the Mind actually is. Beyond any conception which would give it material form and substance and spatial location, Only-Mind simply *is*. And it is No-thing.

*

Before closing this chapter I wish to introduce two additional terms closely associated with Only-Mind, One-Mind, No-thing-Mind, Buddha-Mind, Only-Self, and No-thing-Self. They are Not-Two (Fu-ni)[8] and Not-One (Fu-ichi).[9] Not-Two is a denial of Pluralism; Not-One is a denial of Monism.

Not-Two means there is absolutely no distinction between anything and anything else. In particular, it means there is no distinction between the knowing subject and the objects known. The subject is the object; the object is the subject. The knower is the known; the known is the knower. On the basis of what has been said about Only-Mind, this is quite clear. The Mind creates the contents of its own consciousness just as that magic mirror of which I spoke generates its own "reflections." Thus, Only-Mind is both the knower and what it knows. As you walk along the street and meet a friend, your Mind is fabricating the whole thing. Your body, the sensation of walking, the street you seem to move along, your friend, your words of greeting, all you are thinking and feeling as you meet him is produced in your Mind as a dream is produced. It is as true to say the street is moving past you as to say you are moving along it. You and the

[8]Not-Two: J., Fu-ni 不二. [9]Not-One: J., Fu-ichi 不一.

street are Not-Two. There is no you; there is no street; there is no motion. Your motionless, spaceless Mind is thinking you and the street and your motion along it into existence. Your friend and you are Not-Two. You both are products of your Mind's imagination. Your Mind is everything and everything is No-thing! Zen is absolute Non-dualism.

I want you to notice there is nothing illogical about this. Deductive reasoning moves from major premise to minor premise to conclusion. Zen's major premise is, "Only-Mind is everything and everything is No-thing." A suitable minor premise is, "A subject and an object are things." By the accepted laws of deductive reasoning, the conclusion must follow, "Therefore, Only-Mind is both subject and object; subject and object are not things."

Another proper minor premise to the same major premise is, "You and your friend are things (individual entities)." The logical conclusion to this second syllogism is, "Therefore, Only-Mind is both you and your friend; both you and your friend are not things (not individual entities)." On Zen premises, Not-Two is an altogether rational deduction.

On the presuppositions of Western philosophy, Nonpluralism must be Monism. If reality is not more than one, it must be one. From this Western standpoint, Zen is an absolute Monism. But in its own context, Zen quite reasonably says, "Not-Two, but also Not-One."

Only-Mind is either a thing or it is not a thing. If it is not a thing, it is Not-One. If it is said to be a thing, then the Zen major premise must be applied, namely, "Every thing is No-thing." "Only-Mind is a thing" would be a proper minor premise. The logical conclusion would be, "Only-Mind is No-thing." But if it is No-thing, Only-Mind is Not-One. Either way one looks at it, Only-Mind is Not-One. Just as there are Not-Two, so also there is Not-One.

Nowhere in all existence is there one single thing; this includes One-Mind. Since One-Mind is Not-One, it must be the No-thing-Mind. As I said before, Only-Mind, which is One-Mind, is not a material brain suspended in space like a ball. There is no matter and no space. What Only-Mind is, is utterly inconceivable. All concepts have form and substance and location; Only-Mind has neither form nor substance nor location. All form and substance and location are nothing but thoughts in Only-Mind.

There are Not-Two. There is Not-One.

• 4 •

ALTHOUGH Only-Mind is not a particular, definable thing, everything indicates its character. Since each thing is equally its thought, each thing is not other than Only-Mind. Its character is to conceive the world which is known to itself, that is, the world which is known to "you." In perceiving that world "you" are perceiving Only-Mind itself.

Careful attention to the world projected and to the manner of its projection has led to a fascinating analysis of the activities of Only-Mind called the Eight-Consciousnesses (Has-shiki).[1] Since the Mind has no form or substance, what it *is* cannot be imagined, but what it *does* suggests that it has eight levels upon which it creates the contents of its consciousness. I will not trouble the reader with the Japanese names of the first seven, but for reasons which will be apparent, I will introduce the Sanskrit term for the eighth when I come to it.

[1]Eight-Consciousnesses: J., Has-shiki 八識; literal translation.

The first five levels correspond to the five senses, or rather to the five types of sensation associated with them. The all-important point is that these are not, as in our Western way of thinking, bodily organs by means of which one gains knowledge of a physical environment. The body, its sense organs, and the environment in which it lives are nothing but thought-images in Only-Mind. The first five levels of the consciousness are the "areas" of the Mind which generate the sensations of seeing, hearing, smelling, tasting, and touching. When you see a purple grape, a black dog, a scarlet sunset, your sweetheart's face, these are not objects outside your body reflecting light into your eyes stimulating optic nerves, thereby transmitting impulses to your brain. All the "visible" properties of these things, such as their form and their color, are, as it were, manufactured by Only-Mind on its first level, the Vision-Consciousness. Your eyes, your body, the grape, the dog, the sunset, the face, and every other thing you have ever "seen" and ever will "see" appear in this way.

Likewise, all sounds—from the laughter of a child to the thunder's roar—come into being in the second level of Only-Mind, the Hearing-Consciousness. There is nothing outside the Mind. The smell of coffee and frying bacon, the taste of an apple, the feel of a cold stone in your hand—each is generated at its respective level: the Smell-Consciousness, the Taste-Consciousness, and the Touch-Consciousness.

In addition to the five sensory-experience-producing levels of the consciousness, there is a sixth which brings into being all nonsensory experience, including our thought processes and our emotions. Everything which you think and feel other than the creations of the five sense-levels of the consciousness is brought forth by the sixth, Thought-Consciousness. In the same way that the Seeing-Consciousness makes up the fly in your soup, the Thought-Consciousness engenders your feeling of disgust at seeing it there, brings to your mind the harsh words you resist addressing to the waiter, and creates your thoughts about going to some other restaurant henceforth.

Of course Westerners are already accustomed to consider thought-activities and emotions as being purely mental functions. The point of novelty in Zen is that these thoughts and emotions are not responses to an objective world with the purpose of enabling an individual to make a satisfactory adjustment to his environment. The entire so-called *objective* world is fabricated in the first five levels of consciousness; the entire so-called *subjective* world is produced in the sixth. Thus the distinction between "objective" and "subjective" disappears. For this reason, Zenists quite rationally reject both these terms in describing mental processes. It is significant that they include the sixth level along with the first five in the same category and often refer to them as the Six-Senses.[2] This clearly implies that to Japanese Buddhists, what Occidentals call the five senses are as much purely mental creations as reasoning and emotional experience. In other words, "subjective" and "objective" are Not-Two.

Next above the Six-Senses, which originate everything of which the Only-Mind is conscious, comes the seventh level which I will call the Spectator-Consciousness. This Spectator-Consciousness is particularly interesting, for on its level both Ignorance (Mu-myō) and also Bodhi, the Awakening, occur.

To illustrate the function of this seventh level, let me describe one of the most popular exhibits at California's Disneyland. The visitor enters a large, perfectly circular theater

[2]Six-Senses: J., Rok-kon 六根; literally, "six-roots."

whose wall all the way around is a motion picture screen some twenty-five feet in height. When the movie begins, the spectators find themselves in the center of a 360-degree picture. One sequence which I remember quite vividly takes the viewer on an airplane ride through the Grand Canyon. I had the feeling of actually being in the plane. Looking forward, I could see approaching brightly colored cliffs; looking toward right and left, I could see those portions of the canyon which I would have seen if I were actually passing over them; turning to the rear, I could see the area that had been passed receding into the distance. Being susceptible to motion sickness, I confess the swooping of the airplane produced sensations of nausea so genuine I was afraid I might lose my lunch. Of course I was not actually moving, but standing on a solid floor watching the show. My point is that although one part of my mind knew it was only a show, the experience of being completely surrounded by this graphically visible world was so realistic that other portions of my mind responded to it as if it were actually there.

Let's go a couple of steps beyond even this degree of cinematic realism to one of the fantasies in Aldous Huxley's novel *Brave New World.* A young couple goes to "the feelies." "Feelies" go beyond mere "movies" to add to the picture and the sound both scent and the sensations of bodily touch.

> The house lights went down. . . .
>
> "Take hold of those metal knobs on the arms of your chair," whispered Lenina. "Otherwise you won't get any of the feely effects."
>
> The Savage did as he was told.
>
> . . . then suddenly, dazzling and incomparably more solid-looking than they would have seemed in actual

> flesh and blood, far more real than reality, there stood the stereoscopic images, locked in one another's arms. . .
>
> The Savage started. That sensation on his lips! He lifted a hand to his mouth; the titillation ceased; let his hand fall back on the metal knob; it began again. The scent organ, meanwhile, breathed pure musk.[3]

That ought to be enough to give you the idea. Now suppose you were in the darkened center of a cycloramic theater like the one at Disneyland, but with the additional effects of stereoscopic images, scents, and touch sensations as in Huxley's "feelies." Even if a part of your mind realized it was all just a show being produced by a film running through a projector, the rest of you would be experiencing it as if it were actually there.

But one thing more is necessary to complete this illustration. Imagine you were placed all alone in that theater at birth, strapped in the center with your hands tied to the feelie-knobs. For you, there has never been anything else but the world portrayed on that cycloramic screen. You have never seen the projector itself or any of the mechanisms by which it produces its effects. Under such circumstances, would you not wholeheartedly believe that the show was real? Would you not take it for granted that what you see, hear, taste, and touch is all actually there?

If you are with me this far, you are ready for my explanation of the seventh level of Only-Mind, the Spectator-Consciousness. It is the observer in the darkened center of the cycloramic theater who has been there always. The Spectator-Consciousness is the unseen seer of the contents of the

[3]Aldous Huxley, *Brave New World* (Harmondsworth: Penguin Books Ltd., 1955), pp. 134f.

consciousness generated by Only-Mind's first six levels. The first five create the visual images, the sounds, the scents, the tastes, the sensations of touch; the sixth originates all thoughts and emotions; the seventh is the part of the Mind which sees those images, hears those sounds, is aware of those touch sensations, perceives those thoughts and emotions, and all the rest. This seventh level of the consciousness is the Spectator of everything which takes place in the first six. It is, then, the Ego; it is the "I" in such sentences as the following: "I see the boat." "I hear the music." "I am thinking about you." "I am happy." This "I," like an eye, can never see itself. The Spectator-Consciousness is such an "I." Observing, it is not observed. It is the unseen seeing-point.

As seeing-point, as focal point of awareness, the Spectator-Consciousness has one all-important interpretive function. It can either suppose that the cycloramic feelie is an objective world made up of the many individual entities it perceives on the screen, or it can guess the truth. It can guess that the known world with its separate entities is in fact just a show, just an appearance—that nothing is really there.

Nothing *is* there! If the Spectator were free to go over to the picture screen and touch it, he would find that screen perfectly motionless. People may be walking about, they may speak to one another; the airplane may seem to carry him through the Grand Canyon. Yet, there are no people; there is no speaking; there is no plane, no canyon. As I stood watching the moving pictures which surrounded me at Disneyland, there was that portion of my mind which realized they were only pictures, even while the rest of me was responding to the show as if it were actuality. But if I had been standing there since birth and never known any other world, that same portion of my mind would doubtless have thought it all substantial and quite real. That is the mind-portion which roughly corresponds to the seventh level of Only-Mind, the Spectator-Consciousness.

Now I wish to show that it is at this seventh level that Only-Mind can, as it were, either "misunderstand" or correctly "understand" the true nature of its own contents. When the Spectator-Consciousness mistakenly believes the dreams engendered by Only-Mind's first six levels are material objects in three-dimensional space outside the Mind, it is in the unenlightened condition called Ignorance. The experience of Enlightenment takes place when there is a Turning-Over (Ten-ne)[4] on the level of the Spectator-Consciousness. When this Turning-Over or Revolution or Convulsion of the Spectator-Consciousness occurs, the same feelie keeps on showing, but at that moment comes the realization that it is nothing more than a feelie. At that moment Only-Mind can exclaim to itself, "There is No-thing! Absolutely No-thing! I am everything and everything is No-thing!"

The *Lankavatara Sutra* (*Ryō ga-kyō*) describes this Turning-Over at the seventh level of consciousness:

> When it is completely understood that the external world is nothing but manifestations of one's own mind, a Turning-Over occurs which strikes at the root of the process of discriminating between things. These things are not destroyed, but one has an attitude of freedom toward them.[5]

[4]Turning-Over: J., Ten-ne 轉依; literally, "revolving-dependency." There is a revolution in one's understanding of the nature of reality upon which one depends for existence.

[5]Daisetz T. Suzuki, *Studies in the Lankavatara Sutra* (London: George Routledge & Sons Ltd., 1930), pp. 390f. He gives the Chinese here. I have paraphrased the Chinese for the sake of clarity.

After the Turning-Over, the same feelie keeps on showing, but henceforth the Spectator-Consciousness realizes that the things it beholds upon the screen cannot be discriminated one from the other. They are not three-dimensional things separated by three-dimensional space. Indeed, our illustration of the cycloramic feelie does not go far enough. A complete illustration would have no separation between the observer, the screen, and the projector. Only-Mind is all these things at once. "Your own" Mind is at the same time the Spectator-Consciousness and the first six levels of the consciousness which project not only all sensory experience but also all rational and emotional experience. When, following the Turning-Over, this is fully understood, then you can sit back and enjoy the show perceiving that there is nothing actually out there, that there is nothing to strive for and nothing to fear. Everything is No-thing. This is what the *Lankavatara Sutra* means by saying in the passage quoted above, "These things are not destroyed, but one has an attitude of freedom toward them." Knowing they are not there, you are thereby delivered from all desires related to them: desires to have them, desires to escape them.

This discussion of the first seven levels of the consciousness may have left the impression that Only-Mind, the Buddha-Mind, is like a physical brain with various lobes, each with its own specialized function. Let us be careful to avoid this error. Remember that Only-Mind is also the No-thing-Mind. This analysis is of its functions, not its constitution.

Now comes the eighth and final function of Only-Mind, the Araya-shiki.[6] This Japanese term is a transliteration of

[6]Stored-up-Consciousness: J., Araya-shiki 阿頼耶識; transliteration of Skt. Alaya-vijnana. The English is a literal translation of the Skt.

the Sanskrit, "Alaya-vijnana." At the beginning of the chapter, I mentioned the importance of the technical designation of the eighth level of the consciousness. Most of us have long known the Sanskrit *alaya* without realizing it; that is, we have heard of the towering Himalaya Mountains on the border between India and Tibet. The highest peak of the Himalaya range is the famous Mount Everest. The root meaning of "Him-alaya" is very interesting: *him* means "snow"; *alaya* means "storage place." During the winter the snow piles up on the peaks of those mountains to a great depth. Warmer weather brings thaws which flood the rivers below; avalanches come crashing down. There are glaciers of ice continuously and irresistibly flowing from the heights. On the peaks there is an accumulation of snow which remains all year round.

The "Alaya-vijnana" is the "Alaya-Consciousness." It is, in other words, the "Stored up" consciousness. Just as snow is stored upon the mountains and in due season runs down to bring water and life to the valleys below, so the eighth level of consciousness is that "area" of Only-Mind in which the yet unexperienced sensations, thoughts, and emotions are stored. Down from the Stored-up-Consciousness they flow activating the first six levels which are perceived by the seventh.

Now return with me to the cycloramic, stereoscopic, stereophonic feelies. The moving pictures and other effects are caused by the passage of a film through the single, lighted aperture before the lens of the projector. Above this opening is a giant metal reel upon which many thousands of feet of film are tightly wound; a corresponding reel beneath takes up the film which has already passed before the lens.

The Stored-up-Consciousness is like the film on the upper

reel which has not yet moved to the projecting lens. All the sights and sounds and other sensations yet to be experienced by the lone spectator in the center of the darkened theater are printed on that film. He has no way of knowing what is coming next, no way by which he can alter the pictures printed on the yet unseen portion of the film, no way to change the order in which those pictures will flash upon his sight. Anyone who has seen a motion picture knows how this is. What he is to be shown is already printed and rolled on the reel in the projector before he takes his seat. What he will watch upon the screen for the next couple of hours is the flow of tens of thousands of those previously printed pictures, with accompanying sound track. (In Huxley's feelies, the film also included a scent track, a feeling track, etc.)

It is in the eighth level, the Stored-up-Consciousness, that all the yet unperceived sensations, thoughts, and emotions which constitute the "future" lie latent. Often questioners at my lectures want to know why, if there is nothing but Mind, things happen as they do. Why, for instance, are you now seated in that particular chair, in that body, in that particular room, expecting to do the particular things you have planned? If things are merely thoughts, why can you not at will change yourself into a frog or the president of the United States? Why can you not simply decide to imagine you are riding down the Nile in an exotic barge with Cleopatra by your side, and be there?

According to the Zen view, you could do these things if—and this "if" is the heart of the matter—*if* you could change the order and contents of the Stored-up-Consciousness deliberately. But this is the catch. Like the upper reel of the motion picture projector's film, all the pictures are already "printed" in the Stored-up-Consciousness. The empirical "you" is there along with everything else. The real you is the Spectator-Consciousness, the unseen seer. All you can do is watch those pictures as they come down and are projected upon the screen of the Six-Senses. Having come to the feelie, all you can do is relax and enjoy the show. You have no choice about which film is playing. The rigidity of your environment, the fact that you seem always to be going about in the same body, the fact that you cannot change things to suit yourself—all these mean simply that you, the Spectator-Consciousness, have absolutely no control over the contents of the Stored-up-Consciousness. What the Alaya-Consciousness shows is what you will see. What it contains is fixed and endless. You are strapped to the seat of an eternal feelie!

The things you experience in the feelie can neither harm you nor help you. They can only entertain you. You can be involved in what you see while at the same time remaining as essentially detached as any spectator of any show. Detached involvement! Involved detachment! This is the way of Zen.

As to the question where Only-Mind found the pictures which wait in the Stored-up-Consciousness, they are all its own creations. They are not photographs of things outside Only-Mind. There is No-thing outside the Mind. Only-Mind is everything. Even this analysis of its Eight-Consciousnesses which you have just read is nothing more than what has just been playing in the theater of Only-Mind.

• 5 •

I BELIEVE the reader is now prepared to explore one of the most baffling and also one of the most significant paradoxes of Zen, the Middle-Way (Chū-dō).[1] Utterly unthinkable on Western presuppositions, the Middle-Way is a thoroughly rational conclusion if one starts from those of Zen. It is the Middle-Way between believing that things exist and believing they do not exist. One of the clearest statements of this paradox is found in the Mahayana scripture known as the *Awakening of Faith* (*Kishin Ron*). The Chinese is easy to read even if one knows no Chinese

非	有		非	非	有
Hi	*u*	;	*hi*	*hi*	*u*

Not-Exist; Not-Not-Exist.

In smoother English it becomes, "Things both do not exist and do not not exist."

So far in this book I have been emphasizing the first half: "There is No-thing"; "No-thing exists." There is Only-Mind. Things are merely its thoughts, not material entities. If I left the discussion at this point, the reader would not understand the Middle-Way, but would have been led off it on the side of No-thing-ness, of "Hi-u."

Having shouted, "Nothing is!" at the top of my voice, I must now cry out, "Everything is!" just as loudly. In answer to a seeker's question about the meaning of Zen, a master is likely to hold up his staff, throw hot tea in the seeker's face, strike him with his shoe, or even cut off his finger with a knife. It is the master's way of saying, "This is it!" If you truly know what that staff is, that tea, the show, the knife, the pain, then you understand Zen. To comprehend the actual nature of any one thing is to comprehend all. A staff is only a staff! Tea is only tea!

[1]Middle-Way: J., Chū-dō 中道; literal translation.

Now I beg the reader's patience. I repeat that from the standpoint of Enlightenment there is no logical inconsistency in asserting the non-nonexistence of things after several pages of asserting their nonexistence. Let me put it this way: although nothing exists outside Only-Mind, everything exists—just as it is—within that Mind. To a dreaming mind, what is happening in the dream is quite real. I can still recall a childhood nightmare in which I was playing near a large tree when that tree suddenly started walking toward me on rootlike legs. The stark terror of it lingers to this day. When I awoke crying, mother assured me it was only a dream, but while I dreamed, I was there in that field. The tree was there too, moving toward me across it. I know now that the "I" in that dream, the field, and the walking tree were only figments of my mind, but in the dream, they were to me substantial entities in three-dimensional space. In that dreamworld my fear was both appropriate to the occasion and quite real. With the experience of Satori, Only-Mind wakes *to* the dream, but not *from* the dream. It begins to realize everything is a dream, but goes right on dreaming. Each dream-thing is real *as a dream*! Each is an actual dream!

Furthermore, those dream-things are exactly what they are, not mere Phenomenal shadows of Noumenal things outside the mind. I pointed out that Western philosophical idealists like Kant believe men can only know their conscious impressions of a thing, never the thing itself as it exists outside their minds. The known teacup is nothing like the teacup itself, that swarm of dancing molecules. For Zen, however, the only teacup there is is the one the Mind is dreaming at the moment. A cup is just a cup! A shoe is just a shoe! The whole mystery of Zen is crowded into such simple affirmations.

Hear what is without doubt the most familiar haiku:

An ancient pond;
A frog takes a flying leap—
The sound of water![2]

The perfect silence of an old temple garden is shattered by the single splash of a diving frog. Truly to understand that sound is to understand everything. It is the famous Zen poet Bashō's exposition of Buddha-Reality. A splash is just a splash!

As a dream is not other than the mind which dreams it into existence, so the splash of the frog is not other than the Buddha-Mind. It is not the frog which makes the sound, but Only-Mind. According to the doctrine of the Eight-Consciousnesses, Only-Mind at its second level, the Hearing-Consciousness, created that splash. To know that splash—just as it is—is to know the Buddha-Reality; the splash *is* the Buddha-Mind. It is the One-Mind which splashes. And everything else is the same as that splash. Thus, to understand *it* is to understand *all*.

The result of this understanding is a reverence for everything. Having this Understanding (Chi-e),[3] one can "worship" a grain of sand, a blade of grass, a toad, a Buddha-Image (Butsu-zō),[4] or anything else, as one would worship the Buddha itself. Such things do not merely represent or symbolize the Buddha; they *are* the Buddha!

I believe the meaning of walking the Middle-Way between

[2]The Japanese original is:

古池や	*Furu ike ya*
蛙飛び込む	*Kawazu tobi komu*
水の音	*Mizu no oto*

[3]Understanding: J., Chi-e 智慧. Skt., Prajna. "Chi" for Jnana; "e" for Mati. Intuitive understanding rather than practical wisdom.

[4]Buddha-Image: J., Butsu-zō 佛像; literal translation.

the existence and the nonexistence of things is now clear. "Hi-u; hi hi-u." Things both do not exist and do not not exist. They do not exist as material objects; they do exist as dreams of Only-Mind. Realizing the first leads to detachment; realizing the second leads to involvement. Traveling the Middle-Way means participating to the fullest in everything which happens because one knows that each thing is in fact a dream in the Buddha-Mind. Each act becomes a mysteriously holy thing which can be contemplated with wonder; and yet one is spared radical emotional involvement in anything through the Understanding that No-thing is actually there.

This is the meaning of the verse of Layman P'ang quoted in Chapter 1:

> Divine way,
> Awesome activity:
> To draw water!
> To carry firewood![5]

[5]See note 3 of Chapter 1 for the Chinese.

6

THERE ARE various Zen terms to indicate the simultaneous nonexistence and non-nonexistence of things. One of the most familiar is Kū, meaning Emptiness or Vacantness.[1] Its ideograph is seen on the meter flags of Japanese taxis meaning the cab is unoccupied. To awake to Understanding

[1]Emptiness or Vacantness: J., Kū 空; literal translation. Skt., Sunyata.

is to discover that everything is Empty. The world remains as before, but suddenly everything takes on an ineffable, mystical quality which makes even the simplest object flood the heart with delight.

Hold your hand before your eyes. What a wonder! How marvelous! It is Empty! This doesn't mean that you are holding nothing in it. The amazing Emptiness perceived is the quality of the hand itself. There it is; but it is not there! It is your Mind manifesting itself to itself. What creativity! What ingenuity! To fabricate such an intricate form with its palm lines, swirling fingerprints, pores, the tiny hairs on the back! To conceive those fingernails! What an awesome thing, this Only-Mind! What a conjuror! How does it ever picture forth such complex delicacies of detail?

In such a way, to see anything in its Emptiness is to see it as a clever construct of the Buddha-Mind. What incredible genius to dream up this veined leaf, that wave-webbed sea, those swallows sweeping across the twilight sky. Each and all are mind-magic; each and all are Empty.

Let us repeat the lovely lines, given in Chapter 1, which well express the mood of Emptiness:

> Bamboo shadows sweep
> stairs of stone,
> But the dust on them
> stirs not.[2]

The interaction of things in their Emptiness is like the motion of shadows on stone—there is no friction. In touching, nothing is touched. Every weight is weightless; every pressure is without pressure. Nothing grates on anything in a

[2]For the Chinese original see Footnote 2, Chapter 1.

world of mind-stuff. However vigorously a thing moves in the Emptiness of nondimensional thought, there is no movement. Rather, it is the Mind which moves. Fudaishi, back in the sixth century A.D., observed that it is as true to say a bridge flows, as the stream beneath it. So it is when one knows the Emptiness of bridges and streams. Each is the Only-Mind; flowing is an activity of that Mind. Since nothing is stationary and nothing moves, a bridge can flow in exactly the same way a stream does. All things move as shadows move: no dust is stirred.

In the world of Emptiness, furthermore, it is just as natural, just as reasonable, to hear the clap of one hand as of two. In fact, the Only-Mind can just as easily make the sound of clapping hands with no hand at all; it does this all the time. Hands are not things! Like the splash of Bashō's frog, the sound of clapping hands is the creation of the second level of the Mind, the Hearing-Consciousness. If one thinks that to hear a clap there must be the percussion of palms in an atmosphere to set eardrums vibrating, he is still in Ignorance. All sounds, from a scream to a symphony, are Empty; that is, they are the cunning contrivances of the No-thing-Mind. Heard so, they *are* the Mind.

All experiences, whether they be "subjective" or "objective," are Empty; therefore, Zen has the expression, In-Out-Emptiness (Nai-ge-kū).[3] The *Hannya-Shin-gyō*, Zen's most frequently memorized sutra, puts it most sweepingly: "Everything is Empty" (Go-un kai kū).[4]

[3]In-Out-Emptiness: J., Nai-ge-kū 內外空; literal translation.

[4]"Everything is Empty": J., Go-un kai kū 五蘊皆空. Go-un is Japanese for the Sanskrit, Five Skandhas, the elements which according to Theravadin Buddhism constitute each entity. The quotation thus means that everything including the constituent elements of each thing is Empty.

*

At this point I beg the reader's indulgence to let me guard against a possible misunderstanding by those familiar with the Hindu concept of Maya. Both Buddhist Emptiness and Hindu Maya point to the nonmateriality of things. My Sanskrit-English dictionary defines Maya as "artifice, device, trick; deceit, fraud; . . . illusory image, phantom; illusion (*in the Vedanta = the power which causes the world to appear as really existent and distinct from the universal soul*). . . ."[5] In the sense that it indicates everything is No-thing, Maya parallels Buddhism's Emptiness, but when we consider the emotional connotation of the two terms, they are antithetical. Maya implies Ignorance. Maya denotes not only the nonobjectivity of things, but also the "deceit," the "fraud" of causing one to believe in their objectivity.

Philosophical Hinduism as taught in the *Vedanta* holds that all things are Maya and concludes that they must be avoided. The result is a world-denying asceticism. The earnest Hindu who believes in Maya carefully avoids contact with the sensory world lest he be contaminated by its deceitful appearances. I like to call Maya "negative negation."

By contrast, Buddhist Emptiness is "positive negation." As indicated above, the Enlightened Mind *enjoys* the Emptiness of things. Indeed, it is precisely their Emptiness which allows a Zenist his reverent and enthusiastic involvement in the world's activities while at the same time preserving the tranquility of detachment. Awakened to the Emptiness of everything, the Zen-man can welcome whatever comes his way, just as it is!

[5]Arthur Anthony Macdonell, *A Practical Sanskrit Dictionary with Transliteration, Accentuation, and Etymological Analysis Throughout* (London: Oxford University Press, 1954), p. 226. Italics in the original.

There is a very significant designation for the unlimited acceptability of things in their Emptiness which will make emphatically clear the contrast between the mood of Maya and that of Emptiness. It is True-As-is-ness (Shin-nyo).[6] I will henceforth translate Shin-nyo simply "As-is-ness." As-is-ness means that things just-as-they-are are good. How could it be otherwise since things just-as-they-are are the Buddha-Mind? I remind you of what I said previously about a teacup being the teacup you know and nothing more. There is no Noumenal object outside your mind to which it vaguely corresponds. A teacup is just a teacup; therefore, a teacup is the Mind which thinks it; therefore, a teacup, just-as-it-is, is good. Everything without exception is equally so. This is the significance of the term "As-is-ness."

This glad welcoming of each thing in its As-is-ness is the essence of the experience of Emptiness; an experience diametrically opposite from Maya's world-denying asceticism. The Emptiness, the No-thing-ness of Zen is bright, active, and life-affirming; the deceitfully illusory character of things as depicted by Hindu Maya is dark, escapist, life-denying. Both of these alternative reactions to believing that the empirical environment is not objectively real can be justified rationally. Some have surmised that the two contrasting responses are reflections of the emotional temper of the two types of believers: the Indians tending toward pessimism and abstract thought, the Chinese and Japanese tending toward optimism and pragmatic activism. Such sociological questions are beyond our present scope. All I want to do here is to disassociate Mahayana's Emptiness from Hinduism's Maya in a way that will prevent confusion.

[6]True-As-is-ness: J., Shin-nyo 眞如; literal translation. Skt., Tathata.

• 7 •

STUDENTS of Hinayana or, more properly, Theravadin Buddhism are sometimes unwilling to accept the Mahayana form, of which Zen is a representative, as true Buddhism. Theravada is the type preserved in the Pali language in such countries as Ceylon and is generally thought to be older than Mahayana by Western scholars. One of the fundamental differences between Theravada and Mahayana is that the former appears to be based on philosophical realism, affirming the objective existence of things. It speaks of a universe composed of a ten-layered series of hells and heavens with the earth in between. In these various realms dwell beings who move from one level to another in a series of rebirths, higher or lower on the scale in accordance with the virtues and vices of their previous lives. The endless round of birth-death-rebirth is called Samsara in Sanskrit, Rin-ne or Shō-ji in Japanese.[1] The deeds whose power shapes the form into which one is reborn are Karma (Gō).[2] The entire universe is said to contain a total of Three-Thousand-Realms. These are known in Japanese as simply the Three-Thousand (San-zen).[3]

As a result of its realism, Theravada teaches an austere way of strict self-discipline by which its adherents keep themselves unspotted by the world. For them, the Middle-Way means the path between overindulgence, on the one

[1]Samsara: J., Rin-ne 輪廻 or Shō-ji 生死. Rin-ne is literally, "wheel-turning"; Shō-ji is literally, "birth-death."

[2]Karma: J., Gō 業; literally, "deeds."

[3]The Three-Thousand: J., San-zen 三千; literal translation. Signifies everything in the entire universe.

hand, and extreme asceticism, on the other. Theravadin monks do not marry, do not own property, and otherwise cut themselves off from ordinary life. The salvation they seek is the cessation of rebirths by the rooting out of all desire. They believe that each of all the individual Sentient Beings (Shu-jō)[4] in the universe is composed of Five Elements known in Sanskrit as the Five Skandhas.[5] At death these elements separate; at rebirth the Karma power produced in past lives draws together an appropriate new group of Five Skandhas which might, for instance, form a fish or an ant or a Brahman priest although the being who just died had been a wealthy merchant. With the cessation of desire, the Karma power is dissolved so that upon death there is no rebirth. The state in which the flame of desire is blown out is Nirvana (Ne-han).[6]

The steps by which desire is to be quenched are carefully worked out and are known as the Four Noble Truths (Shi-shō-tai)[7] and the Noble Eightfold Path (Has-shō-dō).[8]

*

This brief summary of Theravadin doctrines was not necessary for most readers perhaps, but since to many people this is what true Buddhism is all about, I want to have these doctrines clearly before the reader. If he is to understand Zen, and for that matter, Mahayana in general, he must

[4]Sentient Beings: J., Shu-jō 衆生; literally, "countless-living."

[5]Five Skandhas: J., Go-un 五蘊; literally, "five piled up." Translation of the Sanskrit, "five-elements."

[6]Nirvana: J., Ne-han 涅槃; transliteration of the Sanskrit. The Sanskrit means "blown out" or "quenched."

[7]Four Noble Truths: J., Shi-shō-tai 四正諦; literal translation.

[8]Noble Eightfold Path: J., Has-shō-dō 八正道; literally, "eight-noble-path."

know the Mahayana interpretation of these doctrines. In most Western textbooks on world religions, it is the Theravadin form which is described. Readers familiar with this sort of Buddhism are disturbed when they hear me saying that the fundamental premise of Zen is "I am everything and everything is No-thing."

Well, friends, hold your hats. I'm going to disturb you a good bit more before I'm through. The fact is, one reason I have felt impelled to write this book is to try to clear up misunderstandings about Mahayana which arise when one tries to interpret it from the standpoint of the apparent realism of Theravada. I say "apparent" because Mahayana thinkers believe the Pali scriptures are correctly understood in terms of No-thing-ness, Emptiness, and the Only-Mind. They hold that the literalists are the mistaken ones.

However that may be, I now come to the main point of this chapter: that according to Mahayana Buddhism, the Three Thousand Realms of existence, the countless Sentient Beings who have been born into them, the Karma which determines the condition into which they are reborn, the Five Skandhas of which each Sentient Being is composed, the Four Noble Truths, the Noble Eightfold Path, the desireless state of Nirvana, and anything else we can think of are all and each absolutely Empty, absolutely No-thing!

One of the most vivid statements of this is found in the *Hannya-Shin-gyō*, which is recited many times daily in Zen temples. I will consider that sutra in some detail in the next two chapters. Just now, I want the reader to look at some Mahayana expressions which help clarify its basic stance regarding the Theravadin world-view.

First, Mahayana asserts that "Samsara is the same as Nirvana." Such a statement is utter nonsense to Theravadins. For them, Samsara and Nirvana are mutually exclusive states of being. For them, salvation means deliverance out of Samsara into Nirvana. "Shō-ji," the Japanese term for Samsara in the present quotation, means literally, "Birth-Death."[9] We noted on a previous page that the continuing round of rebirth and death, rebirth and death is the tedious cycle from which Theravadins long to be free. When the flame of desire is at last extinguished by meticulous self-discipline, Karma power dissolves and the Samsara cycle ceases forever. Following the death of the one who has attained desirelessness, there will be no more rebirths. He has achieved Nirvana.

But Zen says, "Samsara is the same as Nirvana." This is a wholly rational deduction from the premise that Only-Mind is everything and everything is No-thing. Let's put it in syllogistic form to make it clear:

> Only-Mind is everything.
> Birth is something; death is something.
> Therefore, Only-Mind is birth and death.

When you see a baby born, the baby, its mother, and the activity of its being born are dream-creations of Only-Mind on the first five levels of its consciousness. Thus the baby, like everything else, *is* the Mind. If you see someone die, it is the same. Again,

> Everything is No-thing.
> Birth is something; death is something.
> Therefore, birth is No-thing and death is No-thing.

[9]Shō-ji is Birth-Death or Samsara. "Samsara is the same as Nirvana": J., Shō-ji Ne-han byō-dō 生死涅槃平等. Ne-han is Nirvana. Byō-dō is "level-degree" or "the same."

The baby who is born is not a flesh-and-blood object in space. It is not a thing; it is a dream. The same with people who die—with all living things which die.

Nirvana is the state of mind in which it is realized that Only-Mind is both birth and death, and that birth and death are not things. Following Satori, the Mind knows that everything is No-thing; therefore all radical desire, all attachment to things, is put out like a flame. In this Nirvana one has awakened to the fact that all is a dream, but still he goes on dreaming. Knowing that all things are dreams, one is no longer deluded into believing any of them are graspable. One can therefore dwell in the midst of them without the wish to possess some and avoid others. In other words, one lives in the world of Birth-Death while being in the desireless state of Nirvana. Therefore, it is quite reasonable for Zen to say, "Samsara is the same as Nirvana." In fact, this is another way of describing the Middle-Way as understood by Zen. It is the narrow path which runs between the nonexistence and the non-nonexistence of things, producing simultaneously the attitudes of detachment and involvement. Nirvana is detachment; Samsara is involvement. Nirvana and Samsara are Not-Two!

A second expression familiar in Mahayana which reveals its general attitude toward Theravadin doctrine is One-Thought is the Three-Thousand Realms (Ichi-nen; San-zen).[10] I have already said that Three-Thousand (San-zen) is a designation of the entire universe as conceived by Theravada. Beginning with the lowest hell and rising to the highest heaven, there are Ten-Realms (Jik-kai).[11] Each of these in-

[10]One-Thought; Three-Thousand Realms: J., Ichi-nen; San-zen 一念三千; literally, "one-thought; three-thousand."

[11]Ten-Realms: J., Jik-kai 十界; literally, "ten worlds."

cludes the other nine realms, all these have ten factors of being, and each of these one thousand is experienced in three forms. The total is Three-Thousand worlds or conditions into which a Sentient Being can be reborn. As mentioned, his placement and state-of-being are determined by the quality of the combined Karma of all his past lives. The law "As a man sows, so shall he reap" works itself out with mathematical precision.[12] The value of every deed is included.

The Mahayana expression "One-Thought; Three-Thousand" signifies that everything in the Three-Thousand Realms of existence is contained in One-Thought (Ichi-nen). They are each and all thoughts of Only-Mind. The world of Three-Thousand realms is in no sense a material thing objective to the Mind. Each of those particular realms as well as all the beings inhabiting them are dreams of Only-Mind—nothing more, nothing less! Just as no one is born, so there is no world into which he is born. His being born and the world into which he is born are both thought-activities of Only-Mind. This wipes out Theravadin realism.

*

The concept One-Thought (Ichi-nen) adds something to the description of Zen which has not been brought out clearly so far. It does not mean one thought in a series of thoughts which make up a stream of consciousness. Rather, Ichi-nen is the timeless instant of thought which Westerners call "now" or "the present." It is the eternal Now of conscious experience, the infinite moment of awareness. The One-Thought is the total picture caught in a single shutter-click of the Mind. The realization of timelessness is a fundamental aspect of Satori.

[12]New Testament, Galatians 6 : 7.

In Western thought, time is a linear dimension of each thing. A shoe box has length, width, height, and duration in time—four dimensions. Man's experience of time can be pictured as someone striding along a flagstone path. The stone his foot is touching as he walks is the present; those he has already stepped upon are the past; the stones waiting before him yet untrodden are the future. Believing in the material existence of the people and things around him, the Westerner sees them all traveling along the path of time with him. The history of nations is just an extension of the same idea. Time is motion along a line.

In Satori, this notion is completely unmade. By the light of Understanding (Chi-e), it is seen that there is no time-line and no motion along it. There is only a fixed point, the Eternal Now, the Timeless Present. This point corresponds to the lighted frame in a movie projector. Returning to our illustration of the cycloramic feelie, this Now is the momentary picture being seen by the Spectator-Consciousness on the screen of the Six-Senses. Instant by instant new pictures come down from the upper reel of the Stored-up-Consciousness and stop momentarily before the motionless lens of the projector. All that actually can be seen is one still picture at a time. Although it will quickly be replaced by another and another in such rapid succession that there seems to be movement on the screen, for the instant a particular picture is projected it constitutes the whole of knowable reality.

In the same way, if the reader will pause to analyze his own experience of things, he will find that all he can know directly is the present instant. Only that instant of perception is immediately real to you. Everything else is memory and anticipation. And note this: you can only experience memory and anticipation themselves in that Now-instant of consciousness. Wiggle and squirm how you will, you can never budge from that Now! All thoughts of past, present, and future are present thoughts. It can never be otherwise.

How long does a present thought last? Represent it by a tiny grain of sand passing through the neck of an hourglass. You'd have to mark that grain to place the Now. It is shorter than the split second it would take that grain to pass. The Now is in fact shorter than the finest line you could draw on that grain of sand. Now is timeless. And that's where you are: in the center of that dimensionless point of the timeless Now. That is where you are insofar as your conscious life is concerned. You believe the material world—including your empirical self—endures beyond your thoughts, and therefore you derive your concept of linear time from that belief.

Since for Zen, only thoughts exist, it follows that the only reality is the Now of conscious experience. When one thought disappears to be replaced by another, No-thing disappears; so there is no past. Thoughts yet to appear are likewise No-thing; so there is no future. The only existence of past, present, or future things is in the timeless, nondimensional Now-point of knowing. Western time is measured by motion through space. In Zen Understanding, there is neither space nor motion; therefore, time is No-thing.

Of course for Zen, "time" can exist just as the Taj Mahal or the onions in your stew; that is, it exists as a thought in Only-Mind. And like them, it is Empty.

*

All this talk about the Timeless Now has been to clarify the meaning of the expression "One-Thought; Three Thousand." I hope it is now plain that for Zen the Three-Thousand realms and all their inhabitants exist for Only-Mind in the timeless instant of One-Thought. The Samsara universe has no history and no future, but is only extant in the instant of projection before the eyeless eye of the unseen seer, the Spectator-Consciousness of Only-Mind.

• 8 •

THE DANGER that Mahayanists might be tempted to believe in the objective reality of things which are set forth in Theravadin doctrine led, long ago, to the writing of a brief sutra which states most emphatically that all these things are Empty. This sutra, the *Hannya-Shin-gyō*,[1] says that the Theravadin teachings all deal with entities which are not entities, but are No-thing. The importance placed upon understanding this in Zen temples is indicated by the fact that the monks there recite the *Shin-gyō*, as it is familiarly called, several times each day from memory.

Hoping to give the reader a sense of the compactness and force of the Chinese version, in the quotations below I will give the pronunciation of the characters just as chanted by Zen monks in Japan. The sutra is so brief, the whole of it in Chinese will be reproduced at the end of the chapter (p. 73). The ideographs shout from the page a staccato of visual meaning for those who can read them.

One of the *Shin-gyō*'s first and most all-inclusive pronouncements is the one already quoted to the effect that the Skandha elements of which everything is said to be com-

[1]*Hannya-Shin-gyō*: Japanese translation of the Sanskrit title, *Prajnaparamita Hrdaya Sutra*; literally, "Understanding-crossing-over-to-heart sutra."

posed are Empty. It then takes these five elements one by one, showing the No-thing-ness of each:

Shō-ken go-un kai kū.
Illumined-Sight, Five-Skandhas all Empty.

"In Enlightenment it is seen that all Five Skandhas are Empty." This means not only each of the Five but also all sets of the Five. These include everything there is.

The first of the Five Skandhas is "Outward-Appearance," the visible form of a thing:

Shiki fu-i kū;
Outward-Appearance not-other-than Emptiness;
Kū fu-i shiki;
Emptiness not-other-than Outward-Appearance;
Shiki soku ze kū;
Outward-Appearance in-other-words this-very Emptiness;
Kū soku ze shiki.
Emptiness in-other-words this-very Outward-Appearance.

In this way the author of the *Shin-gyō* affirms the Emptiness of the visible form of everything in the whole universe. To make it perfectly clear, he says it four different ways. In smoother English:

> The Outward-Appearance of things is not other than Emptiness; Emptiness is not other than the Outward-Appearance of things; their Outward-Appearance is, in other words, this very Emptiness; Emptiness is, in other words, this very Outward-Appearance.

He then goes on to say precisely the same thing about

each of the remaining four Skandhas: Sense-Perception (Ju), Idea-Conceiving (Sō), Mental-Activities (Gyō), and General-Consciousness (Shiki). You can substitute each of these for "Shiki" in the above and have the complete statement. The first "Shiki" and the fifth are different ideographs giving the respective meanings indicated.

Much could be added about the significance of each of the Five Skandhas; suffice it to say that the author of the *Shin-gyō* has stated as emphatically as possible the belief that all the elements or characteristics of which each and every thing is composed are Empty. This means that everything that ever was or ever will be is Empty. Anyone who may be thinking that the doctrine of the Five Skandhas refers to substantial realities outside Only-Mind is, according to the *Shin-gyō*, still deep in Ignorance.

Its author nails this down with a final all-inclusive dictum:

Ze sho hō kū.
These many particles Empty.

Suzuki translates this line, "All things are here characterized by Emptiness."[2] More literally it says, "Every particle of everything is Empty."

The rest of the sutra is made up of illustrations of this passage as applied to various key doctrines of Theravada. First in the list is the whole Samsara process:

Fu-shō; fu-metsu.
No-birth; no annihilation-of-existence.

[2]Daisetz Teitaro Suzuki, *Essays in Zen Buddhism*, Third Series (London: Rider and Company, 1953), p. 203.

This refers not only to animate, but also to inanimate things. "Nothing comes to be; nothing ceases to be."

Since there is No-thing, the zealous attempts to extinguish the fire of desire by which the heart is contaminated and, thereby, to achieve purity are all meaningless:

Fu-ku; *fu-jō.*
No-contamination; no-purity.

It is this aspect of Zen teaching which allows its priests and monks to marry, live a normal family life, own property, and do other such things which are forbidden to Theravadin monks. Realizing the world is a dream, one has no need to renounce the world. No-thing is defiled; No-thing is pure.

After taking up the Five Skandhas a second time and saying they are all No-thing, the author next comes to a meticulous denial of the objective reality of each of the Six-Senses and all their products:

Mu gen ni bi zetsu shin i;
No-thing: eye, ear, nose, tongue, body, Mind;
Mu shiki shō kō
No-thing: visible-form, sound, fragrance,
mi soku hō;
taste, feeling of touch, doctrines;
Mu gen-kai ni-kai
No-thing: world-of-sight, world-of sound,
bi-kai zetsu-kai shin-kai
world-of-scent, world-of-taste, world-of-touch,
i-shiki-kai.
world-of-thought.

Here by means of threefold repetition the author has shown

the absolute No-thing-ness of the Six-Senses, the experiences they engender, and the worlds they portray. Remembering that the first five include all aspects of the "objective" world and that the Sixth-Sense includes all aspects of the "subjective" world of rational thought, emotion, memory, and so on, it is clear that the *Hannya-Shin-gyō* affirms the Zen doctrine of In-Out-Emptiness (Nai-ge-kū). Subject and object are Not-Two; they are Not-One; they are the contents of Only-Mind; they are No-thing.

Theravada teaches that the purpose of all discipline is the extinction of Ignorance. The *Hannya-Shin-gyō* says:

Mu mu-myō; yaku mu mu-myō jin.
No-thing Ignorance; and No-thing Ignorance extinction.

"Ignorance is No-thing, and also the extinction of Ignorance is No-thing."

Theravada teaches that each thing in all the Three-Thousand-Realms comes into being as a result of a twelvefold chain of causation. The *Hannya-Shin-gyō* relentlessly asserts the No-thing-ness of each of the twelve links beginning with the first, Ignorance, just given, and going on to the others in ascending order. It likewise says that the extinction of each is No-thing. Since the goal of each Theravadin monk is to break this chain which binds him to the Samsara wheel of reincarnation, the *Hannya-Shin-gyō* is saying in effect that the ardent discipline practiced in Theravada is evidence that its followers have not yet attained Enlightenment.

The twelve links are: Ignorance (Mu-myō), Mental Activity (Gyō), Consciousness (Shiki), Name and Visible Form (Myō-shiki), Six-Senses (Roku-nyū), Contact (Shoku), Sense Perception (Ju), Desire (Ai), Attachment (Shu), Being (U), Birth (Shō), Age-Death (Rō-shi).

Any one of the twelve can be inserted into the verse just quoted in the place of Ignorance (Mu-myō). I will do only two more which seem to me of special interest:

Mu ai; yaku mu ai jin.
No-thing desire; and No-thing desire extinction.

The word for Desire (Ai) is the same used in the Japanese Bible for "love" in such passages as "God is love."[3] For Zen, Ignorance of the No-thing-ness of a person such as one's sweetheart or one's child can lead to a radical love-attachment to that person. When Understanding is attained, however, people of all types are freely accepted in their Emptiness, but without any of them exciting that radical love-attachment. Love itself is also welcomed in its Emptiness, that is, as a creation of the Sixth-Sense. In Satori the radical nature of all love-attachments has been dispelled. When watching the feelie, one may vicariously have a sort of love for the child in the show by identifying with the mother. When the child dies, the viewer may even weep as he sits there in the theater. But his grief is not a serious emotion, for he understands that the child he saw there never actually lived. Therefore, Zen can say that both love-attachments and the extinction of love-attachments are No-thing.

Another especially interesting link among the twelve of the causal chain is Existence. It is the same word "u" which was introduced in the expression "Hi-u; hi hi-u" (Not-Exist; Not Not-Exist). Here we read:

Mu u; yaku mu u jin.
No-thing existence; and No-thing existence extinction.

[3]New Testament, 1 John 4 : 8, 16.

"Existence is No-thing; and the extinction of existence is No-thing." To extinguish one's love for another is to dim one's sense of the other's existence. But the *Hannya-Shin-gyō* goes much further than that. That person has no existence. How could his existence be extinguished? No-thing is. Existence itself is nonexistent. For Theravada, entering Nirvana means extinguishing one's own existence. Who never was can never cease to be.

Moving on to the next Theravadin doctrine with which the author of the *Shin-gyō* deals, the reader will come to the familiar Four Noble Truths. These are summarized by four Chinese ideographs: Suffering (Ku), Collection (Shū), Annihilation (Metsu), and Path (Dō).[4] "Collection" signifies the force which brings together the Five Skandhas of which individuals are constituted. The *Shin-gyō* says simply:

Mu	*ku*	*shū*	*metsu*	*dō.*
No-thing:	Suffering,	Collection,	Annihilation,	Path.

In five ideographs, the author denies the objective substantiality of all the matters dealt with in the Four Noble Truths and the Noble-Eightfold-Path which many consider to be the central Theravadin doctrines concerning deliverance. Sakyamuni himself is said to have discovered them at the time of his Enlightenment.

Briefly stated, the Four Noble Truths are: (1) Suffering is a fact of ordinary human existence. (2) It is caused by desire, for so long as one cares about someone or something, threats to their well-being are a potential source of suffering. Think of a mother's agony when her child is seriously ill, a hus-

[4]Suffering: J., Ku 苦; Collection: J., Shū 集; Annihilation: J., Metsu 滅; Path: J., Dō 道.

band's pain when his wife is unfaithful, a wealthy man's uneasiness when financial disaster threatens. Unfulfilled desires produce the pain of frustration. (3) Since all suffering is caused by desire, it follows that the annihilation of desire will result in the cessation of suffering. If a man cares for no one, no one can hurt him. If he is not attached to possessions, their loss is a matter of indifference. (4) The Eightfold-Path is a series of steps by which desire can systematically be eliminated and the peace of Nirvana attained.

Zen agrees with the *Shin-gyō* that desire-born suffering is No-thing; there is no one to do the desiring, No-thing to be desired, and desire itself is a creation of Only-Mind. In accordance with As-is-ness, desire just-as-it-is is good. But as noted above, Enlightened desire is not radical desire. Desire itself is Empty. It is No-thing. This being so, why speak of annihilating it? Why speak of walking an Eightfold-Path toward annihilating it? Suffering itself is Empty and, therefore, good just-as-it-is. It is to be accepted, not eliminated. Like everything else, suffering *is* the Buddha-Mind. The quest for deliverance from suffering is, in this sense, an evidence of Ignorance.

The next items dealt with by the *Shin-gyō*'s author are Understanding and Attainment. The former, already introduced as the insight or wisdom attained in the experience of Satori, is Chi-e, or as here, just Chi. It is the opposite of Ignorance (Mu-myō). The ideograph for Myō is composed of the two chief light sources, the sun and the moon; hence, Ignorance is Not-Light. Understanding is, from the Zen point of view, the illuminating insight gained upon the Turning-Over of the Spectator-Consciousness. It is waking to the fact that one is dreaming while continuing to dream. As an activity of Only-Mind, understanding itself is not a thing which can be sought for and attained.

Attainment (Toku) is the acquiring of Understanding. It is, therefore, a synonym for Enlightenment or Satori. There are many references in Zen literature to the foolishness of the quest for Enlightenment. Those who have attained Satori know there is no Satori to be attained. Both the quest for Understanding and the Attainment of Understanding are nothing more nor less than thought-images in the Buddha-Mind. Therefore, it is not surprising to find the author of the *Hannya-Shin-gyō* writing,

Mu chi; yaku mu toku.
No-thing Understanding; and No-thing Attainment.

"Understanding is No-thing; and Attainment is No-thing." From this Mahayana standpoint, the consecrated efforts of Theravadin monks to walk the Noble-Eightfold-Path, to adhere to their many monkish vows, to do all their tradition requires of them in order that they may attain the Understanding of Enlightenment—all is pointless. However admirable their dedication may seem, misguided zeal is futile. Attachment to Enlightenment is as much a result of Ignorance as any other attachment.

佛說摩訶般若波羅蜜多心經

觀自在菩薩　行深般若波羅蜜多時　照見五蘊皆空　度一切苦厄　舍利子　色不異空　空不異色
色即是空　空即是色　受想行識　亦復如是　舍利子　是諸法空相　不生不滅　不垢不淨　不增
不減　是故空中無色　無受想行識　無眼耳鼻舌身意　無色聲香味觸法　無眼界　乃至無意識界
無無明　亦無無明盡　乃至無老死　亦無老死盡　無苦集滅道　無智亦無得　以無所得故　菩提薩
埵　依般若波羅蜜多故　心無罣礙　無罣礙故　無有恐怖　遠離一切顛倒夢想　究竟涅槃　三世諸
佛　依般若波羅蜜多故　得阿耨多羅三藐三菩提　故知般若波羅蜜多　是大神呪　是大明呪　是無
上呪　是無等等呪　能除一切苦　眞實不虛　故說般若波羅蜜多呪　即說呪曰　揭諦　揭諦　波羅
揭諦　波羅僧揭諦　菩提薩婆訶　般若心經

• 9 •

THERE IS one other expression in the *Hannya-Shin-gyō* which I want to take up separately because it adds something new to my presentation of Zen. The freedom of Only-Mind—your freedom—to enter all Samsara worlds which is implied in the expression "One-Thought; Three-Thousand-Realms" (Ichi-nen; San-zen) is made explicit by the term No-Obstacle (Mu-kei-ge).[1] *Kei* and *ge* are almost synonymous ideographs for "obstacle." The doubling of meaning is a device of the Chinese language to achieve emphasis: "No-thing Obstacle-Obstacle." English would say, "Obstacles are nothing whatsoever." All surfaces, all walls, all boundaries, all wrappings, all skins, all insulating substances by means of which things remain themselves and exclude others are No-thing.

The complete verse in the *Shin-gyō* which contains Mu-kei-ge is this:

Shin mu kei ge;
Mind No-thing Obstacle Obstacle;
mu kei ge ko.
No-thing Obstacle Obstacle because.

"To the Mind all Obstacles are No-thing whatsoever; this is because all Obstacles are No-thing."

[1]No-Obstacle: J., Mu-kei-ge 無罣礙; literally, "No-thing Obstacle-Obstacle." Suzuki gives it a positive translation, "interpenetration," or "perfect intermingling." If there are no separating obstacles it follows that things perfectly interpenetrate one another.

Since one and all of the Three-Thousand-Realms exist in One-Thought, it is quite easy for the Spectator-Consciousness, you yourself, to be in San Francisco one instant and in Tokyo the next. Spatial distances are No-Obstacle to Only-Mind. There is no space, no time. San Francisco and Tokyo are equally dream-stuff. In the case of movie film, there can be a hundred feet of pictures showing purple waves washing up the white beach of Waikiki, and the next hundred feet depicting the Golden Gate Bridge with its towers half hidden in evening fog. Since only pictures are involved, they can be spliced together any way one chooses. Since Only-Mind creates nothing but dream pictures, it can produce those pictures in any sequence it chooses. In the discussion of One-Thought, I pointed out that the timeless instant of the Now is like one photograph in a long series of photographs on a motion picture film. In the Now-moment, that one scene is all that exists. But the dream pictures of Only-Mind are not truly printed on a film which continues to exist after they have been shown. In the split second of the Now, there is that one scene. What went immediately before it has ceased to exist completely. Not even the memory of it remains. What is perceived as a "memory" in the single scene of the Now-instant is as much a creation of that instant as its "present" aspects. If, therefore, in a particular Now-instant you find a "memory" of being in San Francisco just a minute ago, and a "present" of being in Tokyo, *that*, for you, is what has happened. Only *that* Now-instant, *that* One-Thought, with whatever sights and sounds and memories it contains—*that* alone exists. The only past there is, the only present there is—both have their entire being in *that* One-Thought. The next instant *that* past and *that* present have ceased to exist forever. The succeeding scene in the Now-instant could be in an altogether different place and an altogether different time in history. Then *that* would be the whole of reality for you. There is absolutely no way for you to remember what the previous, now nonexistent scene may have been. You see one mind-picture at a time. You see only that one picture. You can never know if there were previous pictures. The single Now-picture contains for you all thoughts of the "past" as well as all experiences of the "present." Being in San Francisco a second ago, or a year ago, or never having been there—all such "memories" are whatever Only-Mind is thinking Now. This One-Thought bears no relationship to anything which happened before. No-thing happened before!

This simply means there are No-Obstacles. In One-Thought, the Mind is anywhere it thinks, and has been anywhere it thinks. In the same way, bodies are No-Obstacle. If the Mind thinks it, you can as easily be a man, a fish, a demon in hell, a deity in heaven, or any being that Mind in its boundless creativity may imagine.

The *Kegon-kyō*[2] develops this principle of No-Obstacle in an especially fascinating way. The state of consciousness of the Enlightened Mind is described metaphorically as a jeweled tower, the Vairochana Tower, in which all the things of which the universe is composed are themselves like jeweled towers. They all interpenetrate one another, for there is No-Obstacle to keep them separate.

Within the Vairochana Tower,

> spacious and exquisitely ornamented, there are also hundreds of thousand of towers beyond all counting.

[2]*Kegon-kyō:* the Japanese title of the *Avatamsaka Sutra*. It is the basic sutra of the Kegon Sect of Buddhism. The portion best known in Japan is the section of it called the *Gandavyuha* translated into Chinese by Pan-jo (759–762).

> Each one of these is as exquisitely ornamented as the main Tower itself. Each is as vast as space.
> And all these towers past calculation in number stand not at all in each other's way; each preserves its individual existence in perfect harmony with all the rest. There is nothing here which bars one tower from being fused with any or all of the others, either individually or collectively. There is a state of perfect intermingling.

The one whose Mind has entered this Tower of Enlightenment "sees himself in all the towers as well as in each single tower; all is contained in one, and each is contained in all."

This is, of course, just a figurative way of saying you can be in San Francisco one minute and in Tokyo the next. There are No-Obstacles such as space, time, and material form to tie you down.

The *Kegon-kyō* not only speaks metaphorically but also describes the Satori-world of No-Obstacles quite explicitly. It says, for instance, that the Tower of Enlightenment is the dwelling place of those

> who make all things enter into One-Thought; who go to any and all lands simply by One-Thought; . . . who perceive in One-Thought any year or all the years in the countless eons of history.

The Tower of Enlightenment is the abode of those

> who, sitting cross-legged and without moving away from their seats, are able to be present simultaneously in all the forms of existence in all the places in the whole universe. . . .
> In one particle of dust is seen the entirety of all lands

> which ever were; . . . and this fusion takes place with No-Obstacle.

Let me end these quotations from the *Kegon Kyō* with a line worth special emphasis: those abiding in the Tower of Enlightenment "perceive that sameness prevails in all beings, in all things!"[3]

The "sameness," the perfect interchangeableness of each thing with every other, brings me back to what I said about being in San Francisco one instant and Tokyo the next. Where there are No-Obstacles, everything is equally accessible. In one of the verses quoted above, you read that while sitting cross-legged, doing Za-zen—without moving from his seat!—one who has experienced Enlightenment can travel to any land, take any form, in the Now-moment of One-Thought.

This is a thoroughly logical deduction from the major premise of Zen. If I am everything, I am also any particular thing. If I am professor of philosophy at Seinan Gakuin University in Fukuoka, Japan, I can as easily be a cat sleeping in the shadow of the Tower of Pisa, or Queen Elizabeth II sitting on the throne of England. I can as easily be William Shakespeare, living in the sixteenth century, or the Japanese emperor Meiji, living in the nineteenth century. All times, all places, all modes of being are equally available to me. There is absolutely No-Obstacle.

If you are wondering, then, why you cannot be in Tokyo

[3]There is a good general discussion of the *Kegon-kyō*, specifically of the *Gandavyuha*, mentioned in footnote 2, in Suzuki, *Essays*, pp. 21–201. Pages 113–37 of this contain his English translation for various selections from the sutra. I have largely followed his translation in the quotations given, but have made a few alterations for the sake of clarity and emphasis. My changes are faithful to the Chinese meaning.

—or Istanbul—next minute and back home again in time for dinner, the Zen answer quite reasonably is "You can! But, you cannot!"

Don't you see? "You," the fellow with the big muscles and the wavy, black hair; "you," the pretty girl with the green eyes and an I.Q. of 135; "you," whatever you're like, are just the same as everything else. "You" are No-thing; "you" are Empty; "you" are one of the dream images in Only-Mind. If the Mind happens to be dreaming "you," there in "your" body, "your" house, in "your" city, with a memory of having been living there for twenty-five years, then, that is just what the Mind is dreaming, and "you" can't change it. Only-Mind dreams what it dreams because it is its nature to dream that dream. "You" have no control over the contents of the dream. The real you is merely the spectator of the dream of which the empirical "you" are a part. All you can do is sit there and watch the show.

• 10 •

THE PREVIOUS two chapters—the one on the *Hannya-Shin-gyō* and the one on No-Obstacle—have emphasized the Not-Exist (Hi-u) side of the Middle-Way. This final chapter of Section I will reaffirm the Not-Not-Exist side (Hi hi-u).

After Satori, one continues to live in the same world, but with new verve and poise. The Middle-Way is not world-denying in the sense that the one who walks it separates himself from the normal activities of daily life. You will recall the quotation from Layman P'ang which glorifies such simple tasks as drawing water and carrying firewood (p. 51).

The world-affirming aspect of Zen is well illustrated in a

series of ten sketches called the Oxherding Pictures.[1] During the twelfth century, Kakuan, a Zen master, did the version I will describe here:

1. Seeking the Ox: the Ox represents Enlightenment. In the first picture, a man is walking along a path, no Ox in sight. The caption beneath the picture indicates that the Ox has never really gone astray, but the Mind which is still in Ignorance cannot see what is right in front of its eyes.
2. Finding the Tracks: here the man is portrayed seeing the prints of the hooves on the path, and beginning to follow them.
3. First Glimpse of the Ox: the hindquarters of the Ox are shown appearing from behind a tree.
4. Catching the Ox: the Ox is pictured pulling back against a rope which is attached to its nose ring.
5. Taming the Ox: the man is seen leading the Ox by the rope, the Ox following docilely.
6. Riding the Ox Home: here he is seated comfortably on the Ox, playing a flute. The accompanying poem is worth quoting:

> Riding free as air he buoyantly comes home
> through evening mists in wide straw-hat and cape.

[1]The Oxherding Pictures are available to Western readers in various forms and versions. The ones I have before me now are: Kapleau, *Three Pillars*, pp. 301–11; Robert O. Ballou, *The Bible of the World* (New York: Viking Press, 1939), pp. 367–376; Zenkei Shibayama, *A Flower Does Not Talk* (Tokyo: Charles E. Tuttle Company, 1970), pp. 152–203. Some picture the Ox as becoming more and more white as the Enlightenment deepens; some stop with the circle. Shibayama gives only six pictures, but the circle is next to last. The many different forms of the series which have been devised simply indicate their effectiveness over the centuries.

Wherever he may go he creates a fresh breeze,
while in his heart profound tranquility prevails.
This Ox requires not a blade of grass.[2]

7. Ox Forgotten, Self Alone: the caption to this picture says in part:

Only on the Ox was he able to come Home,
But lo, the Ox is now vanished, and alone
and serene sits the man.[3]

I said before, the Enlightened Mind knows there is no Enlightenment to be sought. Like everything else, Enlightenment is No-thing. So the Enlightened one is shown sitting alone in his Home looking out the window at the trees and hills of his Native Place. He is the Spectator-Consciousness after the Turning-Over.

8. Both Ox and Self Forgotten: here there is nothing but a circle. Now Only-Mind knows itself in its undifferentiated wholeness. There is neither oneself nor any other thing. Here is portrayed the Non-Exist side of the Middle-Way.

9. Returning to the Source: a sketch of something which I take to be a pine bough extending out over the stump of a plum tree whose branches are in bloom. Having seen itself in its undifferentiated wholeness, the Mind can now look upon the things of the world again with insight into their true nature. The caption ends:

Seated in his hut, he hankers not for things outside.
Streams meander on of themselves,
red flowers naturally bloom red.[4]

[2]Kapleau, *Three Pillars*, p. 307. [3]Ibid., p. 308. [4]Ibid., p. 310.

10. Entering the Market Place with Helping Hands: the picture is of the man, fat and bare-chested, with a big smile on his face, and a large bundle over his shoulder. The caption in poetry reads:

> Barechested, barefooted, he comes into the market place.
> Muddied and dust-covered, how broadly he grins!
> Without recourse to mystic powers,
> withered trees he swiftly brings to bloom.[5]

Back into the marketplace is back into the world of ordinary affairs. The Enlightened one does not try to keep himself pure from the defilements of human existence. He is unconcerned for the mud and dust which cover him. He is ready to take up whatever work there is for him to do. But the grin on his face shows he knows the secret of it all. He can now make trees bloom merely by an act of thought.

In Satori, things do Not-Not-Exist (Hi hi-u). The enlightened Zen-man is actively engaged in ordinary affairs not different from those before the Enlightenment occurred. The Mind does not stop dreaming, it simply has realized that it is dreaming. The world of dreams goes on as before; the only change is coming to know its true nature. This is Understanding (Chi-e). If the experience of Satori had stopped at Picture Eight—the bare circle—it would have been incomplete. The Mind would have remained with the Non-Existence of things and, therefore, would not yet have found the Middle-Way. The ninth and tenth pictures restore the balance by returning to the world of familiar things and ordinary activities.

[5]Ibid., p. 311.

*

There are two Buddhist terms I wish to introduce at this point because they further clarify the world-affirming aspect of Zen Enlightenment. From the standpoint of Western Realism, the two seem unrelated; from the Zen position, they denote the same basic experience, though with slightly different nuances. The terms are: Compassion (Jihi)[6] and No-Thinking (Hi-shi-ryō).[7]

One of the chief reasons Buddhism has been thought by some to teach essentially the same ethic as Christianity is its frequent use of the word Compassion. This is a good example of the sort of semantical problem which arises when a person attempts to translate the ideas of one religion into a language historically rooted in the literature of another religion. The English "compassion" is conditioned by the New Testament concept of emotional involvement in the joys and sorrows of others. The word itself, "com-passion," is from the Latin, meaning to share the feelings of others.

[6]Compassion: J., Jihi 慈悲; literally "affection-sorrow." In its popular use, its meaning is almost identical with the English, "com-passion." Buddhism, however, distinguishes between U-en-no-jihi 有縁の慈悲 and Mu-en-no-jihi 無縁の慈悲. "En" signifies emotional involvement which causes attachments. "U" means existence; "Mu" means non-existence. Buddhism advocates Mu-en-no-jihi; it renounces U-en-no-jihi. In other words, Zen Compassion is "Jihi-without-emotional attachment"; Zen renounces compassion which is "Jihi-in-which-emotional-attachments-exist." Zen Compassion (Mu-en-no-jihi) presupposes that both its subject and its object are No-thing-Selves (Mu-ga). It requires that the subject and the object of the Compassionate relationship are Not-Two.

[7]No-Thinking: J., Hi-shi-ryō 非思量; literally, "no-thinking-amount." It means then, "no amount of thinking" or "no thinking whatsoever."

In Jesus' parable of the Prodigal Son, for example, the sorry spectacle of the son who had wasted his father's gifts and was returning home in rags did not deter the loving father. "While the son was yet at a distance, his father saw him and had compassion, and ran and embraced him and kissed him."[8] For Westerners, whether they are Christian or not, "compassion" is soaked through with the emotion-tone of such biblical narratives as this. When they read of Buddhist Compassion, they assume it means the same.

In fact, while Christian compassion signifies emotional involvement in the joys and sorrows of others, Buddhist Compassion signifies an attitude based on the realization that there are no self, no others, no joys, no sorrows.

Zen Compassion is the feeling of indiscriminate acceptance of anyone and anything which is being encountered in the Now-instant of One-Thought. The background of this feeling is the knowledge of As-is-ness. Its essential difference from Christian compassion is made clear by the fact that it is directed toward inanimate objects in just the same way that it is directed toward people. A Christian can have compassion toward someone who is ill or in trouble, even toward a hungry dog or a wounded cat; but in the Christian context, it is impossible to have compassion toward a clod of earth, a stone, or a river. The semantics of the term simply will not bear this meaning. There must be some sort of fellow feeling grounded on the premise that I am a living creature and the needy other is a living creature.

Zen Compassion is established on the premise that everything is Empty; that is, that everything is a thought in Only-Mind. This being so, everything—just-as-it-is—is good. Everything, as-it-is, is the Buddha-Mind itself. It follows

[8]New Testament, Luke 15 : 20.

that everything is equally acceptable. If one meets a beautifully dressed woman, a filthy beggar, or a Zen master, each is equally welcome. If a thief comes at you with a knife, your mother comes to you with a delicious dinner on her tray, each is equally welcome. If you find a perfect, golden chrysanthemum blooming outside your window, or stub your toe on a fallen log, both the flower and the log are equally welcome. In the context of Satori, Compassion (Jihi) means the tranquil acceptance of everything, just-as-it-is. It is the attitude of absolute impartiality. In the previous chapter, I quoted a line from the *Kegon-kyō* stating that the principle of sameness prevails in all things. Since everything is the Buddha-Mind, everything is of identical worth. Only one who is still in Ignorance would prefer some things to others, some people to others, some modes of conduct to others. Buddhist Compassion welcomes everything and every living being without discrimination.

This indicates plainly what the ninth and tenth Oxherding Pictures show in their own way; namely, that following Enlightenment, there is no mud which must be washed away or no dust which needs to be brushed off to achieve perfect purity. One can enter the marketplace where all sorts of people and all manner of activities will be encountered, without prejudice or dismay or disgust or condescension toward any. Zen Compassion is the total acceptance of being. It is the absolute rejection of all value judgments.

Alongside this Compassion, I wish to place the other concept, No-Thinking (Hi-shi-ryō). It designates a state of mind which allows one to act without self-conscious thought. One simply does what he does without thinking about it. Anyone who has cultivated a manual skill like playing golf or the piano knows how awkward he can become when he stops to analyze what he is doing. I am no pianist, but back in high school days I memorized one short classical piece. Some thirty years later, I can still sit down to the piano and come forth with it *if* I don't stop and consciously try to think what comes next. As soon as I start thinking about it, I'm lost.

Again, I have known fellows who are pretty good golfers until they start reading some book on how to improve their strokes. When they just walk up to the ball and swing spontaneously, they may send it a couple of hundred yards in the general direction of the cup. But when they pause and begin to think whether the grip is right, whether they are bending the proper knee, whether the left foot is pointing where it should, they suddenly become all thumbs. A mighty swing, and the ball dribbles a few feet over behind a bush!

This sort of self-conscious, thought-encumbered action is the opposite of Zen's No-Thinking. No-Thinking is spontaneity. A good example from Zen is the sport of Jūdō,[9] which means literally, "flexible way." One faces an opponent without fear or hindering thoughts about how that opponent will attack or how one will counter his attack. One's actions are relaxed, free-flowing, and unpremeditated. Such No-Thinking activity is poised and natural. It has an uninhibited grace about it. Anyone who has watched Heifetz play the violin has a sense of what No-Thinking must be like.

Western realists achieve this spontaneous mastery of their instrument through practice; true Zenists do everything this way simply by letting Only-Mind be itself. In Satori, there is only the Mind moving freely, with No-thing to hinder. Self-conscious thoughts about how to do this or that are born of

[9]Jūdō 柔道; literally, "flexible-way," or "pliable-way." It is a form of Zen wrestling well known in the West. *Jū* can mean "weakness; gentleness; softness; tenderness."

Ignorance. What the Mind does, it does out of itself naturally. Even if the One-Thought includes doing something awkwardly, it is the graceful, poised unembarrassed awkwardness of No-Thinking.

You see now the similarity of attitude manifested in Zen Compassion and in Zen No-Thinking. The Compassion accepts everything just-as-it-is, without tension, with perfectly uninhibited freedom. This Compassion does not think about hows and whys and whens and wheres. It takes things as they come, with equal serenity towards all. Acting with No-Thinking is the same. Without thinking about the why, the how, the where, the when of what you are doing, you simply do it. Deeds of No-Thinking are deeds of Compassion. Compassion accepts everything with no questions; No-Thought does everything with no questions.

Thus I bring Section I to a close with a strong assertion of the practical, activistic, world-affirming side of the Middle-Way. But obviously one cannot take a step on this Not-Not-Exist side in the freedom of Compassion and of No-Thinking without stepping just as firmly on the Not-Exist side. To walk the Middle-Way is to live in the world involved in its activities as if things have being and, at the same time, to live detached from everything as if it were without being.

When it is believed that Only-Mind is everything and everything is No-thing, this Middle-Way is the single path reason will allow.

SECTION

SOME PERSONAL EXPERIENCES IN BUDDHIST TEMPLES

· 11 ·

THE PREVIOUS section was an introduction to Zen's basic premises and some of its terminology. In Section II, I will describe a series of personal experiences in Buddhist temples which illustrate how the implications of these premises are applied in contemporary Japan. Some twenty years in that country engaged in teaching world religions and philosophy of religion have given me both the opportunity and the incentive to spend much of my time with Buddhist priests and teachers. What follows are a few samples of the sort of thing I have enjoyed doing.

Each chapter of Section II will center on happenings in one particular temple. Most of these are Zen temples located in the Kyoto area. Exceptions will be noted in the chapters concerned. Since the Japanese word for Buddhist temple[1] is *-ji*, the names of the temples will not include the redundancy of the English word. For example, I will say "Nanzen-ji," not "Nanzenji Temple."

The reader should understand that a particular temple usually includes several large, wooden buildings—worship halls, teaching halls, meditation halls, living quarters for monks and masters, and such. These are often situated within acres of forests, gardens, lakes, streams, waterfalls, and

[1]Buddhist temple: J., *-ji* 寺; literally, just "temple," but it always means a Buddhist temple. When the ideograph stands by itself it is read *tera.*

other natural adornments. Such holdings are many centuries old, and although the original buildings have in many cases been destroyed by fire, even the present restorations are quite ancient. The gardens are frequently the work of some noted designer of a bygone age as famous for his skill as a gifted painter or sculptor might be.

*

Let us return to Nanzen-ji and the incident with which I opened Chapter 1. It was twilight. I had been reading for a couple of hours high up beside the open trough of the moss-covered brick aqueduct whose waters flow above the temple grounds. Climbing down the hill I heard the whispering of giant trees blended with the murmurs of the stream over my head. Burning pine needles perfumed the air. I made my way past the darkened hulk of the Main Hall seeking the source of the scent.

There, a red glow. Beside it a black-robed monk like an animated extension of the deepening darkness raked the fallen needles to feed the flame. The sound of the bamboo prongs through the sand . . .

Standing near for some moments of silence, at last I bowed and spoke. "The tree shadows taste of pine smoke," I said. We watched its noiseless ascent into the night. I asked then, "What is your intention in Zen?"

His reply was immediate: "To be this smoke."

*

Exactly. Only-Mind is everything. In Satori, the monk and the smoke are Not-Two.

*

On another occasion, a formal interview had been arranged for me with Nanzen-ji's famous master, Abbot Zenkei Shibayama. I was led by a young monk to a small room in the Abbot's residence where I waited seated on the *tatami* (mat floor). The monk served tea on a low table, the room's only furnishing. Through the opened wall-panels there was a view of green foliage and grey stone.

The Abbot, a man perhaps in his middle sixties with a beautifully tranquil face, entered and took his place across the table bidding me gracious welcome. There followed a delicious hour and a half of soft-spoken conversation about his faith. Toward the end he summoned the novice monk who, upon his master's request, brought a square of heavy paper on which a few lines of charcoal ink suggested a white cloud floating.

Putting it into my hand, he said, "This is every question about Zen, and every answer."

I have it still.

*

A single cloud moving silent in space; an ink impression of such a cloud—neither is more real nor less real than the other. Each is precisely the same thing because each is Nothing; and each, just as it is, is the Buddha-Mind. To have this Understanding, and to live it, is to walk the Middle-Way. This is the Alpha and the Omega of Zen.

*

Pure and fresh are the flowers with dew,
Clear and bright is the singing of the birds;
Clouds are calm, waters are blue.
Who has written the True Word of no letters?
Lofty are the mountains, green are the trees,
Deep are the valleys, lucid are the streams;

The wind is soft, the moon is serene.
Calmly I read the True Word of no letters.[2]

—Zenkei Shibayama

[2]Zenkei Shibayama, *A Flower Does Not Talk, Zen Essays* (Tokyo: Charles E. Tuttle Company, 1970), p. 264.

• 12 •

ONE OF the favorite tourist attractions in Kyoto is the spectacularly lovely Kinkaku-ji (Golden-Pavilion-Temple). In the form of a two-storied pagoda, her slate roofs are arched bird wings soaring. Her brightly gilded sides are luminous lace. She stands like a female Narcissus, gazing upon herself in a mirror-lake at her feet.

A few years ago a psychotic young man became convinced the Golden Pavilion had bewitched him with her beauty and made him her slave. Believing he could only regain his freedom by destroying her, he set fire to her and she burned to the ground. This factual incident became the seed of a novel by Yukio Mishima called, in its English translation, *The Temple of the Golden Pavilion.* Just before the young man's deed of arson the following thoughts fill his mind:

> When the Golden Temple reflected the evening sun or shone in the moon, it was the light of the water that made the entire structure look as if it were mysteriously floating along and flapping its wings. The strong bonds of the temple's form were loosened by the reflection of the quivering water, and at such moments the Golden Temple seemed to be constructed

> of materials like wind and water and flame that are constantly in motion.
>
> The beauty of the Golden Temple was unsurpassed. And I knew now where my great weariness had come from. That beauty was taking a last chance to exercise its power over me and to bind me with that impotence which had so often overcome me in the past.[1]

It is a strange tale full of the mood of Zen, and well worth reading.

*

I have spent many tranquil hours gazing upon the perfectly restored form of this delight and have a favorite vantage point across the lake where I install myself. A couple of hundred feet to the left of the Golden Pavilion is the Main Hall of the temple compound. One afternoon, following a half hour or so in my favorite spot, I walked over to the Main Hall and called out asking admittance. A middle-aged monk kindly invited me in, and we were soon earnestly engaged in talking of Zen.

I raised the question of the nature of Buddha-Reality. He abruptly stood to his feet, beckoned me to follow, led me through the building into a large room whose whole side was open to a view of the Golden Pavilion. He took in the scene with a wide sweep of his arm. This was his wordless answer to my query.

We sat then, looking. At last I said, "Is it not true that there are two Golden Pavilions, both equally real, but the lower one more real than the upper?"

[1]Yukio Mishima, *The Temple of the Golden Pavilion*, trans. Ivan Morris (Tokyo: Charles E. Tuttle Company, 1959), p. 256.

His eyes turned sharply upon me and he spoke with such spontaneity that he slipped into informal Japanese: "*Bikkuri shita! Wakatta na!*" (I am surprised! You understand, don't you!).

Thus he approved my comment.

*

From the position of Satori, both the Pavilion of gilded wood standing upon the bank, and the shimmering, rippling reflection of it in the water, are equally real. Each is an image in Only-Mind. But since the fragile, dancing mirror-form is more obviously No-thing, it is the more real of two equally real which are in fact Not-Two. The ripple-image is more apparently what it truly is than the solid-structure-image. It is visibly Empty. But this lake-vision is every bit as real—and real in just the same way—as the land-Pavilion. Things both do not exist, and do not not exist. "Hi-u; hi hi-u!"

• 13 •

ALTHOUGH I have been there many times since, I shall never forget my first visit to the world-renowned garden of sand and large stones at the upper edge of the vast grounds of Ryōan-ji. Through ignorance of the visiting hours, I arrived after the garden had been closed to the public for the day. Falling into conversation with a young monk strolling the lower path, I was delighted when he offered to open the door and let me in for a private viewing.

One goes through a short, roofed hallway to an open veranda. There, enclosed on three sides with an aged clay wall which itself is an object of esthetic potency, lies a small, flat garden consisting solely of raked white sand with fifteen big stones of varying shapes sitting starkly here and there upon it. That late afternoon I was allowed the unusual privilege of solitary contemplation. During public hours, visitors troop through the building by the hundreds. On a subsequent visit I heard a Western tourist exclaim, "Is that all there is to it?"

Yes. That's all there is. And from the Zen view, that is absolutely *all there is*! To see the garden of Ryōan-ji with the eyes of Enlightenment is to see the whole of the universe.

Ignorance looks upon it as sand and rocks outside the mind. The grains of sand and the individual rocks are thought by Western science to be individual swarms of molecules beyond the capacity of the senses to perceive. They are unknowable Noumena. The sensory perception of these things—their form, their surface texture, their color—constitute their appearance as Phenomena. Thus does the Ignorance of Occidental Realism view the scene.

Through the eyes of Enlightenment, however, Ryōan-ji's garden is variously looked upon as a wide sea with islands here and there, as an extended cloud through which mountain peaks protrude, as a mother tiger with her cubs—or simply as sand and rocks. Since space and substance are totally an invention of Only-Mind, the dimensions of the garden and the identity of its objects can be anything the Mind conceives them to be. In accord with the *Kegon-kyō*'s doctrine of No-Obstacle, anything can be any other thing, or everything. Moving from one image to another—from sand and stones to sea and islands, to clouds and peaks, to tiger and cubs, back to sand and stones—the consciousness is led to a deepened experience of No-thing-ness, of Emptiness, of the nonobjectivity of the scene. The Mind is thus more completely liberated from notions of material size, shape, and substance. Ultimately, the clearest vision of the garden is to see simply sand and rocks, just as they are, with no distinction between Phenomena and Noumena. The beholder and the beheld are Not-Two.

*

That evening in solitary contemplation of Ryōan-ji's marvel, I saw it from the Zen perspective. I knew in myself that special flavor on the tongue of the Mind, the taste of Zen.

*

On a subsequent visit, I found to the rear of the building which faces the garden just described, another tiny one of moss, small trees, a pool, and a round stone basin about a foot in diameter. The hollowed-out center of this basin is square. It is surrounded by four Chinese ideographs in such a way that the square becomes a component of each, like this:

Read clockwise, beginning with the top, we have: 吾唯足知. In Japanese pronunciation, this becomes:

Ware tada taru o shiru.
I only sufficiency know.

"I know only sufficiency." In other words, "I lack nothing." This is a verbal statement of the experience one has while viewing Ryōan-ji's garden of stones and sand. The enclosing circle represents Only-Mind. Within it, everything, just as it is, is good. From the standpoint of the As-is-ness of things, there cannot be either too little or too much. The entire universe of Three-Thousand-Realms is the creation of the first six levels of the consciousness as programmed by the Eighth and observed by the Seventh. Nothing either should be or could be more or less than it is. Everything is exactly right. The Buddha-Mind knows only "sufficiency."

• 14 •

I'LL RELATE two things which happened at Myōshin-ji on the same afternoon. First, while I was viewing a large, disk-shaped mirror on the altar of one of its numerous halls, a monk entered and stood beside me. After a while I asked, "Why does one polish dust from the mirror?"

Now this was a leading question. To polish the mirror is an expression for emptying the consciousness of all its images. Particular thought-pictures are likened to specks of dust which must be wiped away. It is similar to turning off the feelie-projector temporarily and looking at the empty screen. It is a state of Mind in which one becomes conscious of consciousness alone. To achieve this undifferentiated Mind-state is a primary objective of doing Za-zen (Sitting-Meditation). The flow of the stream of consciousness is stopped for a while to allow the Mind to behold itself in its absolute Emptiness.

I return to my question put to the monk: "Why does one polish dust from the mirror?"

After some moments, the answer came: "Great-Teacher Enō knows!"

Enō was the Sixth Patriarch of the Zen School in China (d. A.D. 713). When his predecessor, the Fifth Patriarch named Kōnin, had a poetry contest for the novices in his temple, the most promising disciple wrote:

> The body is the Enlightenment-Tree;
> The Mind is like the stand of a bright mirror.
> Time and again, time and again
> strive to polish, to wipe it,
> That no dust accumulate.[1]

Kōnin preferred this poem to all the others submitted and was about to announce that he had chosen its author to succeed him and become the Sixth Patriarch.

Then someone showed him another poem which had been written anonymously on one of the monastery walls:

> The essence of Enlightenment is that
> a tree is No-thing.
> The Mind-Mirror, furthermore, has no stand.

[1]Author's translation of:
身 是 菩 提 樹／心 如 明 鏡 臺
時 時 勤 拂 拭／莫 使 惹 塵 挨

Fundamentally, there is not one single thing.
How, then, could dust accumulate?[2]

Kōnin investigated and at last found the author to be an illiterate servant in the monastery kitchen named Enō. Enō's poem had been written on the wall for him by a fellow servant. Kōnin continued to see much merit in the first poem, but saw in Enō's a still deeper grasp of Buddha-Reality. For this reason, to the surprise of many, he chose the illiterate Enō to be the next Patriarch instead of the well-educated composer of the first poem.

The Sudden-Enlightenment school of Zen, called Rinzai in Japanese, follows the Sixth Patriarch, Enō. The Gradual-Enlightenment school, Sōtō, follows the learned monk who wrote the first poem. Sōtō seeks a gradually deepening insight by repeated practice of Za-zen and through the study of Zen sutras and other writings. It polishes the mirror. The Rinzai school, however, is suspicious of talk about mirrors and dust and polishing. Its adherents believe that the crucial Realization comes all at once and once for all. The experience can be repeated perhaps, but the initial Awakening is the moment of truth. Once the Spectator-Consciousness has gone through the trauma of the Turning-Over, things will never be the same again. Things will never *be* again; things will henceforth be the Buddha-Mind.

To my question about polishing the mirror, the monk at Myōshin-ji, a Rinzai temple, replied, "Great-Teacher Daishi knows!" He was thereby opting for Enō's view of things. Here again is the third line of his poem:

[2]Author's translation of:
菩 提 本 無 樹／心 鏡 亦 非 臺
本 來 無 一 物／何 處 惹 塵 埃

本　　來　　無　　一　　物
Essence (Origin) / come / No-thing / one / thing.

You can translate it for yourself: "Coming from the essence or origin of being, not one single thing!" or "Essentially, there is not one single thing!"

From this we see that the Satori exclamation of Kapleau, "There is nothing! Absolutely nothing!" which I have mentioned several times, was right in line with Zen tradition. He all but quoted the words of Zen's Sixth Patriarch written more than a thousand years ago.

*

Following my encounter with Myōshin-ji's monk who spoke of Enō, I made a very interesting mistake. Roaming through several of the buildings there, I unintentionally went to the special entrance used only for novices seeking admittance for extended training. Stepping inside, I called out the usual Japanese greeting, "*Gomen kudasai!*"

Silence. I tried again.

Suddenly the very air around me began to tremble as a thunder-like voice roared out one word: "D-A-A-A-A-A-A-A-R-R-R-E-E-E-E-E-E-E?" It meant "WHO?"

There are several Zen anecdotes of men who experienced Satori when asked under unusual and stressful circumstances the simple question, "Who are you?" The appropriate answer is not, of course, "Joe Jones from Brooklyn."

To discover one's true identity is to realize that "Joe Jones" is a No-thing-Self, and that "Brooklyn" is No-thing. The proper response to the question, "Who are you?" is an awakening to the fact of Only-Mind; it is the realization that the Buddha-Mind is everything and that everything is No-thing. At the probing word "WHO . . . ?" the Spectator-Consciousness may be shocked into the Understanding that the world is a feelie projected by the Six-Senses from the reel of the Stored-Up-Consciousness. This Zen Awakening to a knowledge of one's own true identity is sometimes called "the discovery of your original face before you were born."

By inadvertently entering the wrong door, I had been treated to that "WHO?" which reverberated through me like a lion's roar. It gave me goose pimples.

I might add that the monks quickly discovered that the fellow at the entrance was not a proper novice. Someone came out and very graciously explained my mistake. I apologized, and left.

It happened some ten years ago, but in the ear of my memory, that mighty voice thunders still.

• 15 •

JUST NORTH of the Go-sho, the Imperial Palace Grounds in Kyoto, is Shōkoku-ji. Let me here give public thanks to one of the priests of this temple, Sohaku Ogata, for his many kindnesses. Some reading this may have seen his book *Zen for the West*, written in English.[1] Through that book I had known of him before I moved to Kyoto. Under his direction, there has been for several years in one of Shōkoku-ji's halls a center for assisting foreigners who come to Japan in search of an understanding of Zen. A portion of the building is his

[1]Sohaku Ogata, *Zen for the West* (New York: Dial Press, 1959). The book includes such things as a Zen interpretation of the *Tao Te Ching*, a new translation of the *Mu-Mon Kan*, etc.

family residence; another portion contains Japanese-style tatami rooms where guests can live as they study. There is also a worship chamber which is used for ritual and for doing Za-zen. From my first visit to him, he was continually generous to me. For several months he received me weekly for a discussion of Zen subjects. He was particularly helpful in locating hard-to-find Chinese passages in Zen literature which until then I had seen only in English translation. For six months during 1966, he provided me a room in his temple where I spent every other night, and many hours daily in Zen studies.

Having had a stroke some years ago, he was slightly paralyzed and was often not feeling well. Nevertheless, he was an unfailingly congenial host to a stream of visitors from Europe and America. For example, Alan Watts, known in the United States as an author of books on Zen, conducted a series of seminars for the tour group he was taking through the Orient in Ogata's worship hall while I was staying there.

I have in a previous chapter said I feel a strong sense of moral obligation to set forth the Zen position in such a way that Japanese Buddhists like Ogata can give wholehearted assent to what I am saying. I have a "materialistic" Western-style liking for this man.

The particular thing I wish to relate concerning Ogata has to do with his life-style. He has a gracious wife and several fine children. His son was about to graduate from high school and was making application to various universities when I lived in the temple. The family life was rich with mutual affection and good humor. Not only Ogata, but all his family joined in showing hospitality to the many guests who came their way.

I would often find a beautiful flower or a piece of fruit

placed in my room by thoughtful hands. Frequently I was invited to enjoy the refreshment of the family bath. It would be impossible to recount the many small, unexpected acts of friendliness shown me by first one and then another of the Ogatas. And with it all, there was a thoughtfulness which did not intrude upon my privacy.

*

As important as any of the experiences related in Section II, here is a practical demonstration of what it means to live believing "I am everything and everything is No-thing." In all I have described, Ogata was acting in accord with this premise. From the viewpoint of his own Satori, I, his other visitors, the members of his family, and his own body with its ailments were each and every one "not a single thing." Therefore, he could relate to them all with ease and total lack of encumbering emotional involvement. He readily accepted all who came his way in their As-is-ness, met them with the warmth of encountering the Buddha-Mind itself. To him they *were* that Mind.

Almost all Buddhist priests in Japan are married and have children. This is in sharp contrast to Theravadin Buddhism in such countries as Ceylon, where even if one has been married before entering monastic life, he leaves his family "to wander lonely as a rhinoceros" in ascetic self-denial. By breaking off personal relationships, the Theravadin hopes to root out all affections and attachments. Sakyamuni, the Indian Founder of Buddhism, himself set such an example.

From the Mahayana position as held by Zen and most types of Buddhism in Japan, however, withdrawal from human relationships shows lack of robust belief in the substance of the Understanding attained in Enlightenment. If the Zen insight is steadily held, then family affection, the pleasures of sexual activity, and all the comforts of a normal home life can be accepted, just as they are, as activities of Only-Mind.

Ogata's genial hospitality and his family relationships are fine illustrations of Buddhist Compassion (Jihi) toward all Sentient-Beings. This Compassion is presented in many of the great Mahayana sutras as the inseparable companion of Understanding (Chi-e). Understanding perceives that no one is an objectively existing individual, that everyone is a thought-image in Only-Mind. The mood of Compassion is the natural and logical response to this Understanding. If everyone you meet is known by you to be an activity of the Buddha-Mind, be that person saint or sinner, beautiful or ugly, friend or foe, you can accept him just as he is. There is no need to avoid emotional attachments when they arise, for these attachments themselves are the product of the Mind. Knowing this, one is not attached to these attachments. All such things are experienced as being Empty and thus can be enjoyed without reservation.

*

When the Zen attitude indicated by the word Jihi (Compassion) is thus understood, a problem which perplexes some Western students of Mahayana is readily solved. Much of its literature emphasizes that a true Bodhi-sattva (Enlightened-Being-ness)[2] makes a vow to save all Sentient-Beings along with himself. The very word Maha-yana (Large Vehicle)[3] implies that Mahayana Buddhism is a Pure-Land-bound wagon capacious enough to carry everyone.

[2]Bodhi-sattva (Enlightened-Being-ness) is the Sanskrit term. The Japanese is Bo-satsu 菩薩, a transliteration of the Sanskrit.

[3]Maha-yana (Large-Vehicle) is the Sanskrit term. The Japanese is Dai-jō 大乘; literal translation.

But how can everyone be carried to the Pure Land if Only-Mind is everyone and everyone is no one? Who are the multitudes of Sentient-Beings a Compassionate Bodhisattva vows to take with him into Enlightenment, if there is Only-Mind?

In the light of what has been said about Understanding and Compassion, I believe the answer is already quite clear. Every living being is, in fact, the Buddha-Mind. In the Realization of this fact, every living being comes to be known for what it truly is. In Enlightenment, therefore, all beings become what they already are, the Buddha. They have never been anything else. For a Bodhisattva, in his great Compassion, to bring all beings to Buddhahood means that the Buddha-Mind accepts everything, just as it is, to be itself. The Buddha is everyone and everyone is no one. The Buddha is everything and everything is not a single thing.

This is repeatedly stated in the *Kongo-kyō* (*Diamond Sutra*). I have before me a beautiful old copy on rice paper. Here is a pertinent passage:

> As thus immeasurable, numberless, limitless Sentient-Beings are delivered, yet in fact the Sentient-Beings to be delivered are No-thing. How is this? . . . If there is to a Bodhisattva such a thing as his own individual entity, the individual entity of other people, the individual entity of Sentient-Beings, the individual entity of some eternal deity, he is not a Bodhisattva.[4]

[4]I will not take the space to give the Chinese ideographs, but for Japanese readers, here is the Japanese pronunciation of the passage I have translated from the *Kongo-kyō*. The English translation is mine. *Metsudō mu-ryō, mushu, mu-hen shujō. Jitsu mu shujō toku metsudō. Nani yue, Shubodai?. . . Moshi Bosatsu u ga-sō, nin-sō, shujō-sō, jushasō—soku—hi Bosatsu.*

I have translated so literally, it makes awkward English, but I hope the blunt force of the Chinese comes through. The three ideographs indicating the incalculable number of beings which are delivered to Enlightenment reinforce one another to give the impression of everything in all worlds. The Bodhisattva saves each and every one. Yet, the author of the *Kongo-kyō* hastens to add, all these beings who are delivered are No-thing.

Realizing the irrationality of this statement from the point of view of unenlightened materialism, he continues: "How can such a strange thing be said? Well, it's like this. If a Bodhisattva believes there are such things as his own empirical self, empirical animate or inanimate beings of any kind, if he believes in the objective existence of anything, he is not a Bodhisattva after all."

It is precisely through realizing he is everything and everything is No-thing, that a Bodhisattva experiences Compassion toward everything. The Enlightened, the Bodhisattva, delivers all beings by realizing that they are nothing more nor less than himself. This "himself" is, of course, not an individual person, but is Only-Mind.

• 16 •

BEHIND the Main Hall of Daitoku-ji is an exquisite little residence temple with a tiny garden, a small Meditation-Hall (Zen-dō), and a fine library of books on Zen in many languages. During my years in Kyoto, all this was presided over by Mrs. Ruth Sasaki, a large, gentle American woman who reminded me of my grandmother. She had some years before married the priest of the temple and, following his death, remained to further his work of introducing Zen to Westerners. Under her auspices numerous Zen materials have been translated into English and published in the name of The First Zen Institute, which she conducted both in Japan and in America.

Most of my training in and practice of Za-zen (Sitting-Meditation) took place in her Zen-dō under the tutelage of various monks of Daitoku-ji's monastery. It was one of their missionary activities to teach foreigners like myself.

The term Zen[1] is Japanese for the Sanskrit Dhyana, and is usually rendered into English by the word Meditation. As in other cases previously noted, the popular connotation of the English is quite different from the Sanskrit-Chinese-Japanese concept it is supposed to translate. In English, to meditate generally means to ponder something, to think carefully about a matter. The objective in Zen Meditation is just the opposite. In Za-zen, the goal is to empty the Mind of all thoughts. This Meditation is a means of stopping the activities of the first six levels of the consciousness—sensory, emotional, and intellectual experience—and contemplating Only-Mind in its absolute Emptiness. It is becoming conscious of consciousness alone.

The technique of sitting cross-legged with palms upward resting on your soles, thumb-tips gently touching, back erect, earlobes in line with the shoulders, nose-tip in line with the navel, eyes partially closed and looking at the ground a few feet in front—this technique aids one to experience a sense of integrated wholeness. To find the correct posture for the backbone, the sitter sways slightly until

[1]J., Zen 禪; more or less literal translation of the Sanskrit Dhyana, usually translated "meditation." But it is not meditating on some subject of interest.

that position can be felt. It is much like balancing a broom handle on the palm of the hand. When the proper posture is found, one seems to float effortlessly. There is no need for the support of a chair back.

A Kōan—an anecdote like the one relating Jōshū's reply to the question whether or not a dog has the Buddha-Nature—is used as a focal point of thought to bring the normal stream of consciousness to a halt. The finale comes when even this concentration point is erased and nothing at all is left on the screen of the consciousness. This gives Only-Mind an undifferentiated vision of itself.

Although the contents of the Mind are No-thing, so long as things *seem* to be, there is the temptation to believe they *are*. Once these thought-images are suppressed and the imageless consciousness itself is observed, then the true nature of "things" is realized.

Imagine a man who has always lived in a remote jungle village and is placed all of a sudden in the seat of a theater with the latest giant movie screen. Seeing a mammoth lion stalking toward him, hearing its monstrous roar, this observer would doubtless flee for his life. Why such radical emotional response? He believes the lion is actually there.

The sophisticated city dwellers would also have a pleasurable tingle of fear at the lion's approach, but they would not try to run away. Why? They know it is not actually there.

What would be the easiest way to show the terrified visitor there is nothing to fear? Just have the projectionist turn off the pictures to enable the viewer to see that nothing is really there but the screen. After this, the movie could be resumed and he could thenceforth watch it with enjoyment. His emotional involvement would then be merely pleasurable, not radical.

This is essentially what happens in Za-zen. Once the

empty screen of the consciousness has been seen, particular images can be allowed to fill it once more. They will never again provoke the beholder to radical emotional involvement. He can enjoy the show with the assurance that there is No-thing to fear and, for that matter, No-thing not to fear. Everything is not a single thing.

I am grateful to those monks whose patience helped me to learn to do Za-zen in spite of my long, inflexible, Western legs. Although she has since passed away, I will never forget the kindness of Ruth Sasaki.

• 17 •

SAIHŌ-JI, better known by its nickname, Koke-dera (Moss Temple), is out past Arashi-yama far on the western edge of Greater Kyoto. With a minimum of buildings, the whole rolling landscape included within its bounds was developed by the gardener-priest Musō Kokushi (1275–1351). It was his intention to make its spacious garden a pictorial representation of Only-Mind. The entire area is covered with a deep carpet of green moss. In its center is a large pond in a shape suggesting the Chinese ideograph for Mind 心. The moss cushion is shadowed by the branches of many towering trees. From time to time the general hush is shattered by a single sharp sound as tangible as a pistol shot. This is caused by a section of bamboo about three feet in length and of large diameter which has been set into the slender stream which feeds the pond. This bamboo pipe is balanced on a frame like a see-saw in such a way that it slowly fills until the water's weight causes it to tilt downward to empty and then to drop back with a loud plop.

The garden depicts the universe emanating from within Only-Mind. To the beholder the Emptiness of things is made mysteriously palpable.

> Velvet moss, gray stone,
> Polished pewter mirror-pond.
> Sudden sound! Silence![1]

Everything there is an inducement to Satori. To know what that sound is, what that silence, what that pond, that stone, that moss is, is to awaken to Understanding.

*

As I wandered Koke-dera's path one morning savoring its mood, I came upon a monk busily sweeping the path with a broom made of a bundle of straw. He hailed me with a boisterous "*Ohayō gozaimasu*" not usual in reserved Japan.

"But, Sir," I responded as if we had already been in long conversation about it, "I continue to ask if there is no Buddha-Image here?"

He laughed heartily. With an impish grin on his face he said, "Is it not known? I burned the Buddha long ago!"

It was obvious he referred to the familiar tale of a Chinese monk named Tan-hsia (Japanese: Tanka), A.D. 738–824.

One cold winter night while staying in a temple in the royal city of the Tang dynasty, he took a wooden image of Buddha off the altar and made a fire of it to warm himself. As he settled down to enjoy the cheerful blaze, the temple custodian came storming up to him shouting rebukes. At this, Tanka began poking about in the ashes.

[1]An original haiku poem: the form of the haiku is five syllables / seven syllables / five syllables, a total of seventeen syllables.

When the near-apoplectic custodian had composed himself enough to ask what on earth he was looking for, Tanka calmly replied, "Why, the Buddha's bones, of course."

"But there'll be no bones," the other man sniffed with exasperation.

"Then hand me down another image to burn," smiled Tanka.

Again and again, the question whether Tanka should have burned the Buddha-Image has been subject for discussion in Zen temples. The deeply Enlightened reply is, in effect, "Why not?"

There in Koke-dera's silver-green shadows, the monk had said it again: "Is it not known? I burned the Buddha long ago!"

In using the informal first person pronoun "I" (Japanese: *boku*), he was identifying himself with Tanka. That Chinese monk of the Tang dynasty and the monk before me on the moss-bordered path were Not-Two. Since both those men, and all Buddha-Images, and the burning or not burning of any particular Buddha-Image are every one "not a single thing," they are to be welcomed in their As-is-ness. Everything, just as it is, is good; that is, everything, just as it is, *is* the Buddha. Burning the Buddha *is* the Buddha.

A Buddha-Image is No-thing, and it is the Buddha. It is not just an image, for all images are thoughts of Only-Mind. The Mind and its thoughts are Not-Two. A Buddha-Image *is* the Buddha, therefore, in just the same way that the moss, the Mind-ideograph pond, the tree shadows, the stones, the sharp report of the dropped bamboo pipe are the Buddha.

A piece of firewood gathered from a forest is as much the Buddha as any temple image. If either is burned, No-thing is burned. The wood and the burning are activities not outside the Buddha-Mind. The Buddha burned the Buddha. There is no deed which is not the Buddha's deed.

This illustrates the amoral character of Buddha-Reality. From the standpoint of Satori, no type of conduct is qualitatively different from any other. Everything—every single thing—is the Buddha. But when one who has Understanding finds himself making some strong moral condemnation of another's act—as, for example, if his child has been murdered or his most valuable treasure stolen—he realizes that those feelings of moral indignation are themselves nothing other than products of Only-Mind. The same is true when he feels guilt and shame for some unkindness he has shown toward another. Such feelings are as much the Buddha as the unkind deed, the self, and the other. Moral judgments are real in the same way dreams are real. While such things do not relate to objective entities, they nevertheless exist as the stuff of consciousness. The Enlightened one is thus able to experience scorn at "evil" conduct and praise at "good" conduct, while realizing that in fact both evil and good are No-thing.

• 18 •

IN ORDER to show that the presuppositions of Zen are shared by other branches of Mahayana Buddhism which superficially viewed seem quite different, I will tell of a visit to Higashi Hongan-ji. It is the headquarters of the most popular sect of Japanese Buddhism, Jōdo-Shin-Shū (True-Pure-Land-Sect). At first glance, its teachings appear to be so similar to Christianity that some have tried, unsuccessfully I think, to trace deliberate borrowings during its earlier history.

Shinran, founder of the True-Pure-Land-Sect,[1] promises birth into the Pure Land of Amida Buddha by simple trust in Amida's Compassionate Vow to save all beings no matter how sinful. In Buddhism, this way of receiving Enlightenment by faith in the power of a Compassionate Savior is contrasted to the way of achieving Enlightenment by self-discipline; that is, the way of Other-Power (Ta-riki) is contrasted to the way of Self-Power (Ji-riki).[2] Following one genuine experience of lifting the heart in trust to the Other-Power, the remainder of one's life is spent in glad Thanksgiving.[3] From that moment, whatever happens—be it pleasant or unpleasant—is perceived to be a gift of Amida and therefore is to be welcomed just as it is. This uninterrupted flow of joyful gratitude is verbally expressed by a ceaseless repetition, either orally or mentally, of the

[1]There are a number of special terms used in the Pure Land Sects largely derived from the *Muryōju-kyō*, the *Kammuryōju-kyō*, and the *Amida-kyō*, the three chief sutras which describe Amida Buddha's Vows, his Pure Land, etc. Shinran, the founder of the True-Pure-Land-Sect in Japan, emphasized the idea that entry into the Pure Land is assured by one genuine act of trust in Amida; his older contemporary and teacher, Hōnen, is said to have laid more emphasis upon reciting the name of Amida, making it a kind of religious practice necessary to the achievement of final birth into the Pure Land. In terms of Christian theology, Hōnen is thought by many to have advocated salvation by works, while Shinran taught salvation by faith alone. There is no space in my present book to introduce the terms and discuss the doctrines of the Pure-Land-Sect in any detail.

[2]Other-Power: J., Ta-riki 他力; Self-Power: J., Ji-riki, 自力. Both are literal translations. For adherents of the Pure Land sects, Amida Buddha is the Other-Power.

[3]Thanksgiving or Thankfulness: J., Kan-sha 感謝; literally, "feel-thanks."

phrase, Namu-Amida-Butsu ("Thanks be to Amida Buddha" or "Adoration to Amida Buddha").[4] Whatever the meaning of the original Sanskrit term *namas*, for the followers of Jōdo-Shin-Shū *namu* expresses the mood of faith in Amida: "I put my trust in Amida Buddha."

Back around 1954, I began to correspond with Saizō Inagaki, the author of a book I had found in Tokyo's Tsukiji Hongan-ji called *Shinran Shōnin's Tanni-shō with Buddhist Psalms*.[5] Since that publication he has shared in the preparation of the English translation of other scriptures of Jōdo-Shin-Shū. He was for some time principal of a large Buddhist high school in the city of Kobe. About twenty years my senior, he nevertheless became a warm friend.

On the particular occasion I want to describe, he had arranged for me to spend a couple of nights at a laymen's retreat held at Higashi Hongan-ji in Kyoto and in fact came along with me. There were some four hundred men from Nagasaki temples participating at that particular time. We rose early and went into the Amida Hall. I tape-recorded their unison chanting of the phrase, Namu-Amida-Butsu, as they sat before the gilt Amida-Image in a standing position on the altar. This was done with changing rhythms and inflections and variations of volume under the direction of a chant-leader up front waving his arms to mark the time. It is not my purpose here to relate how we later washed the

[4]Namu-Amida-Butsu 南無阿彌陀佛; literally, "adore-Amida-Buddha." The Sanskrit name for which Amida is a transliteration of Amitābha, meaning Infinite-Light.

[5]Saizō Inagaki, *Shinran Shōnin's Tanni-shō with Buddhist Psalms* (Toyonaka: Eishinsha, 1949). The Psalms mentioned in the title are his own original poems of which the quotation given is a sample. The English indicates his familiarity with Christian hymns and the King James Bible.

floors on our knees with buckets and scrub brushes, and attended lectures and discussion groups led by noted Jōdo-Shin scholars. I wish to stop with the experience of chanting the Nem-Butsu (Think-Buddha, the designation for repeating Namu-Amida-Butsu)[6] before the Amida-Image, and my conversation with Inagaki just after.

As we were walking together from the Amida Hall that early morning I asked him, "Do these men believe the spirit of Amida somehow animates the golden image? Do they think he actually hears their Nem-Butsu?"

Inagaki replied, "You're thinking of idol worship. Do you remember the poem I wrote setting forth my own feelings when I do Nem-Butsu before an Amida-zō?"

I remembered. And I will quote his poem for you here:

> O Amitābha, thou art hid from my sinful eye:
> Thou art Spirit: thou art the Law:
> Thou art invisible: yet I embrace thee by faith
> Through thy strong Son of immortal love—Sakyamuni!
> When I think of thee and thy grace,
> Thou takest to thyself a spiritual form and presentest
> Thyself before mine eyes—a beautiful image,
> Noble and holy, august and supreme.
> I see thy face, not with eyes, but in vision;
> The image that I adore and worship is golden and of human form;
> That image is not a mere symbol of thee, much less an idol
> Though it is made of wood or of metal by hand of man.

[6]Nem-Butsu 念佛; literally, "think Buddha." Repeating Namu-Amida-Butsu is to Think-Buddha, is to feel Thankfulness to Amida.

I stand in thy presence day and night before thy image:
I fold my hands before thy face and worship, but not as an idol-worshipper.
Thou art here and there, in the air, and in the earth:
Thou art anywhere; everywhere is thy mansion in the heights above and in the depths beneath.
Thou abidest in my heart: thy kingdom is built in my faith:
When I hear thy commandment and thy Promise,
Thou appearest before me: showest thyself to the eye of my mind.
Rejoiced am I to be given thy image:
A wooden image, a golden image, a painted image, or a metal image.
There is no difference for me: always I am before thee, Amitābha, my Saviour.
Let the world say that I am foolish to worship an idol
That is made of clay or of wood, a work of man's hand.
Let them cry and despise me, and call me by the name of idolater,
Yet I never did grasp my Master by scientific understanding, nor by materialistic symbol:
Thy image is my Lord: my Lord comes before me in an image within my soul.
Clay is clay, but the clay in thy form is the Saviour himself, and not the clay of earth.[7]

It is apparent that Inagaki does not make a real distinction between himself as worshipper, the image of Amida before which he worships, and the unseen, all-compassionate Ami-

[7]Inagaki, *Tanni-shō*, pp. 49–51.

da Spirit. He uses personalistic and materialistic forms as metaphors to describe that which is essentially indescribable and ineffable. The technical term for such usages is Hō-ben (Method of Convenience).[8] It is somewhat similar to the concept of Myth made popular by the Christian theologian Rudolf Bultmann. These Myths or Hōben are useful teaching devices to give graspable substance to realities which are ultimately beyond the capacity of speech to express. When the Jōdo-Shin doctrines are "demythologized," they are found to embody the same concepts of Buddha-Reality and rest upon the same presuppositions as Zen.

Although the vocabulary and mode of describing the experience of Enlightenment used by Inagaki is quite different from that used by Zen masters, the experience itself is essentially the same.

In his own existential realization of Only-Mind, Inagaki delights to think of it in the form of an image of Buddha. Whether it is conceived as being of wood or gold or clay or pure mind-stuff makes no difference. These images are not symbols of Amida, they *are* Amida. And according to his experience Inagaki himself is not other than they: he is not other than Amida. Amida is not other than the Buddha-Mind, Only-Mind. Inagaki, therefore, quite rightly denies that he is an idol worshipper. A true idol worshipper is someone who offers adoration to a deity other than himself which is in some sense present in the image before which he is prostrated. Although in terms of Hōben Inagaki can say, "I fold my hands before thy face and worship," he adds, "but

[8]Hō-ben 方便; literally, "method-convenient." It is a translation of the Sanskrit, Upaya. It is a teaching device in which things not actually true are used to lead the seeker to the experience of Enlightenment.

not as an idol-worshipper." Such prepositions as "before" which imply otherness are accommodated language. He comes nearer to the demythologized statement of his experience when he says, "Thy kingdom is built in my faith." On the level of Hōben, it is permissible to speak of a distinction between Self-Power (Ji-riki) and Other-Power (Ta-riki).[9] Ultimately, the Self is the Other and the Other is the Self. Both Self and Other are No-thing-Selves (Mu-ga).

The life-tone following the dawning of true faith which makes one aware of the luminous presence of Amida in everything is not different from that of realizing joyfully the Emptiness of all things. It is not accidental that the Indian Buddhist philosopher Nagarjuna, who wrote much about Emptiness and the Middle-Way between the existence and nonexistence of things, is recognized by Jōdo-Shin as its Founding Father, the First Patriarch. The attitude of Thankfulness for all things whether they seem good or bad is not different from that of Zen-Compassion already discussed. The belief that everything without exception is a gift of Amida is not other than the belief that everything is a thought-image created in Only-Mind. Come poverty or wealth, come sickness or health, come foe or friend—he who trusts in Amida says, "*Arigatō gozaimasu!*" (literally, "Something wonderful there is"). This is to believe that everything, just as it is, is the Buddha-Mind, and therefore everything, just as it is, is good. It is the same as realizing that Only-Mind is everything, and everything is No-thing.

Entering Amida's Pure Land is not different from experiencing Nirvana in Samsara. The Pure Land is a mythological statement or Hōben for the experience of Satori depicted in the last of the Oxherding Pictures, where the Enlightened

[9]See note 2 above.

One is back in the market place with a grin upon his face.

No less an authority on Japanese Buddhism than Daisetz Teitaro Suzuki, himself a Rinzai Zenist, says that there are more genuine cases of Satori among the believers in Jōdo-Shin than in Zen. The element of trust in Amidaism lies in the fact that its adherents do not need to empty the screen of the consciousness and see it in its undifferentiated state with their own eyes, as it were. People who practice Za-zen sometimes achieve that direct vision of the absolute Emptiness of the Mind, but it is a great effort. Jōdo-Shin believers can achieve the attitude of indiscriminate Thankfulness for all things which is the hallmark of genuine Enlightenment without ever putting aside the Hōben of Amida, his Compassionate Vow to save all who trust in him, and his Pure Land. Since this experience itself is the totality of genuine Enlightenment, the route by which it is reached does not matter. One way is as good as another so long as one arrives.

If the reader is interested in a detailed and carefully documented presentation of the essential oneness of Zen and Jōdo-Shin, I invite him to read my book called *Japanese Buddhism and Christianity*.[10] All I want to do in this present chapter is to make clearer the Zen experience by letting it be seen from another perspective. The heart of it is welcoming the world in all its aspects, whether this be described as limitless Thankfulness to Amida, as Compassion toward everything, or as realizing that things both do not and do not not exist through the Turning-Over at the level of the Spectator-Consciousness.

[10]Tucker N. Callaway, *Japanese Buddhism and Christianity* (Tokyo: Shinkyo Shuppan-sha, 1957), especially Chapter III.

• 19 •

TO GIVE a still different perspective I wish to speak of the great Tōdai-ji of Nara. It is the headquarters of the almost extinct Kegon Sect of Buddhism. In my opinion there could be few places on earth more lovely than the thousands of acres of enormous trees, hills, streams, lakes, and other natural beauties included within its confines.

For a number of years while living in Kyoto, I commuted each week to teach English literature, my hobby, at Nara Joshi Daigaku, one of the oldest and best-known universities for women in all Japan. My classes were scheduled on two consecutive days, so I would usually spend the night in an inn near the terminal of the Keihan-shin electric train. Consequently, I have roamed the trails and halls of Nara's Buddhist temples and Shinto shrines all hours of the day and night. I have seen Tōdai-ji by twilight, by moonlight, by dawn's gold—seen her in all her many moods.

But let me take myself in hand and get to the subject. One morning I fell into conversation with a priest who was sitting at a booth just within the entrance to Tōdai-ji's Hall of the Great Buddha, selling souvenirs to the tourists. We stood there dwarfed by the colossal form of Birushana Buddha seated on a broad, bronze lotus blossom. The image is said to be 53½ feet high and to weigh 452 tons! Its face alone is 16 feet from chin to hairline! Its ears are 8½ feet from lobe to tip! Being somewhat familiar with the *Kegon-kyō* (Sanskrit: *Avatamsaka Sutra* or *Garland of Flowers Sutra*), the chief sutra of the Kegon Sect, I was able to ask a few leading questions of the priest in the souvenir stand. He seemed pleasantly surprised to find that this long-legged foreigner with the big nose, the bald head, and the fat belly could not only speak Japanese, but seemed to know a little about Buddhism. He told me his name, and it was my turn to be surprised. He was one of the top men in the Tōdai-ji hierarchy. Due to the friendship begun that day, I was soon to be granted some rare privileges seldom enjoyed by outsiders.

For instance, on a night of the annual festival of the Taking-of-the-Sacred-Water (O-mizutori) which is celebrated only in Tōdai-ji but is known nation-wide, he took me along with him right into the heart of things. He let me accompany him into the preparation rooms where monks had been fasting and meditating for days to ready themselves for their participation in the exotic rituals involved. Already Holy Water had been drawn from the nearby Sacred Well which is enclosed in its own special house. This building is opened but once a year, during O-mizutori. As I watched, a team of these monks began, one at a time at about fifteen-minute intervals, to shoulder a long bamboo pole with a bundle of dried straw tied to its top end and to run up the long flight of stone steps leading to the Second-Month-Hall (Nigatsu-dō) high on the hill above. I watched as this bundle was ignited just before the successive monks sprinted up the stairs. As they ran, flames and sparks streamed out behind them.

On the hillslope below the veranda which circled the Second-Month-Hall, more than five thousand spectators from all over Japan were gathered to view this famous night-spectacle. As a running monk reached the veranda, he would continue his dash completely around the Hall with sparks spewing in all directions into the darkness. At this, the crowd would surge forward, each person trying to let some of the falling sparks touch his own body. The popular belief is that those seared by the flames of Tōdai-ji during the O-mizutori festival will have all misfortune-causing evil forces burned away. By this rite of purification, they hope to have a year of prosperity free from illness and other calamities.

The finale of the special evening I am describing took place well after midnight within the Second-Month-Hall itself in an area which is closed to the general public. There, beside my respected friend, I sat with a large group of monks to watch a strange ritual-dance whose tradition goes back many generations. Robed priests wearing tall wooden clogs moved in unison this way and that, often leaping high into the air and causing a deafening clatter on the thick board flooring. From time to time they would seize bundles of straw, ignite them, and throw them about on the floor. The structure was made entirely of wood. It was incredible that the whole thing did not go up in flames. Centuries ago enemies had tried to burn the Second-Month-Hall, but the fire was quenched in a seemingly miraculous way. The exotic dance I beheld was to celebrate that deliverance.

Behind the dancers is a sealed wooden shaft about ten feet square which runs from floor to ceiling. No man now living has ever seen what is enclosed within that shaft, but it is believed there are two images of Kannon, the Buddha of Compassion. One of these is said by tradition to be only seven inches tall and always warm to the touch; the other, seven feet high and of surpassing beauty. The ritual dance is an act of praise to Kannon who is invisibly present within the closed shaft.

As we were watching I asked my guide, "Would you please tell me your own feeling regarding the hidden Kannon? Since she is reputedly lovely, would it not be well to open the shaft and let her be seen?"

He smiled, but did not speak for some time. I thought perhaps it was too intimate a question to receive a reply. But he said, "Is she not more lovely to me unseen? Could anything be more beautiful than my mind-image of what is there concealed? Could anything be more real? It is better so."

I indicated above that Tōdai-ji is the headquarters of the Kegon Sect. You will recall quotations from its chief scripture, the *Kegon-kyō*, in an earlier chapter setting forth the doctrine of No-Obstacle (Mu-keige). According to this teaching, each thing is any other thing, or all other things, because everything is No-thing. My companion, as a highly placed teacher of this sect, was steeped in the study of the *Kegon-kyō*. At appropriate times, he and his fellow priests would do ceremonial obeisance to the hulking form of Birushana sitting within what is claimed to be the largest wooden building in the world far below the Second-Month-Hall at the bottom of the hill. But his heart's preference was for the invisible Kannon of the Second-Month-Hall.

In the fifth chapter of the *Kegon-kyō* is the following: "In every particle of dust are numberless Buddhas. The entirety of the Buddha land is visible on the tip of one hair." Thus viewed, a Buddha made of tons of bronze is no more substantial than an unseen Buddha uncertainly suspected of standing within a tightly sealed shaft of heavy boards. What is "seen" is not seen; what is not "seen" is plainly seen. Only-Mind creates the nonobjective world of sight in its Seeing-Consciousness. All objects of the visible world are Empty.

Side by side with their study of the *Kegon-kyō*, with its subtle concept of interpenetrating jeweled towers of Enlightenment expounded in its doctrine of No-Obstacle, and its other philosophical profundities such as the idea of the timeless One-Thought, the priests and monks of Tōdai-ji make extravagant use of what some might call crude magical practices.

This has been suggested in my account of the O-mizutori festival with its offer of good fortune through contact with cleansing sparks. During normal, nonfestal days at the Second-Month-Hall, I have several times observed a priest piling up a dozen or so short, white sticks log-cabin fashion on a metal tray on top of a small altar at the rear of the shaft enclosing the invisible Kannon images. Next, he would set fire to them and chant the *Kegon-kyō* as they were consumed by the flames. Each of the sticks, about five inches in length, had previously had someone's wish written on it in charcoal ink: a wish to be cured of some illness, a wish for a successful business transaction, for a happy marriage, and for other such things. As these wish-sticks were transformed into fire and smoke, the petitioners felt that their inscribed desires were being received by the concealed Kannon just behind the shaft panel.

There are several other devices at the Second-Month-Hall for making wishes come true. These are for the people who flock there expecting tangible benefits, but who have little or no understanding of the *Kegon-kyō* in its true meaning.

The whole is presided over by men like my friend who dwell within the Birushana Tower of Enlightenment, where one thing is all things and all things are one thing because there is No-thing. To them the unseen Kannon is more real than the gigantic bronze form of Birushana down the hill in the same way that the lake's reflection of the Golden Pavilion is more real to the Zen monks of Kinkaku-ji than the equally real building of wood and gilt paint standing on the bank. For Tōdai-ji's genuine adherents, the language of the *Kegon-kyō* is more satisfying than the abrupt quips and conundrums of Zen, but the ultimate experience behind the two very different "religious" styles is easily recognizable as the same.

*

It is generally true of the various temples of all the Buddhist sects in Japan that popular practice is largely concerned with banishing bad-luck-bringing forces and calling up those forces which promote prosperity and well-being. Each sect emphasizes some particular sutra or group of sutras and has its characteristic Hōben or mythological representations which over the years have produced distinctive ceremonies, art, literature, and life-styles. Of the many lay people who take part in the temple rituals, only a small percent have a grasp of the inner significance of the faith they profess. For those who have gone behind the Hōben to the experiential substance, however, there is no real difference between the various sects. All forms of Mahayana Buddhism are talking about the same thing in different vocabulary.

*

While I'm into this matter of the popular forms of Buddhism, it may be well to add that one reason students of Buddhism in its Mahayana forms are easily led astray is that it can be discussed on two levels. Buddhists themselves easily slip from one to the other and back again a dozen times during a single conversation. One gradually gets an intuitive feel for these shifts just as one gets a sense of the balance necessary to ride a bicycle. At the beginning these shifts can be quite bewildering. Buddhism has technical terms to denote these two levels of comprehension: True-Truth (Shin-tai) and Popular-Truth (Zoku-tai).[1] When one

[1]True-Truth: J., Shin-tai 眞諦; literal translation. Shin-tai means Absolute Truth, Ultimate Truth, the Truth which is the content of Understanding, the Truth which is perceived in Enlightenment.

Popular-Truth: J., Zoku-tai 俗諦. *Zoku* means popular or vulgar or

has experienced Enlightenment and can exclaim with Understanding, "Only-Mind is everything and everything is Nothing!"—when he can genuinely feel Compassion toward everything just as it is, he is living in accordance with True-Truth. When, however, he distinguishes between himself and others, when he still believes that some things are more desirable than others, when he still believes three-dimensional things exist in three-dimensional space, he is on the level of Popular-Truth. One of my Buddhist dictionaries distinguishes between Shin-tai and Zoku-tai in the following quotation. It calls Shin-tai and Zoku-tai respectively:

> the ultimate aspect of truth and secular aspect of truth. . . . The latter aspect can be regarded as relative and temporary, the former as absolute and permanent. Therefore, from the former standpoint the ultimate aspect is real, the secular aspect is illusory. Comparing both, from the ultimate viewpoint everything is equal and void [Empty], while from the secular viewpoint everything is different from every other thing and existent.[2]

When discussing Buddhist thought and practice, even the most deeply Enlightened Buddhists will freely make use of Hōben, myth, and the vocabulary of Popular-Truth. If the

---

crude; by extension it can be said to mean mundane, worldly, secular, etc. In Buddhism, Zoku-tai is the sort of understanding held by those still in Ignorance. Zoku-tai believes in a material universe composed of separate things and particular individuals. Even while speaking of Shin-tai, language forces one to express himself in the communication forms of Zoku-tai.

[2]*Japanese-English Buddhist Dictionary* (Tokyo: Daitō Shuppan-sha, 1965), p. 287.

investigator has not developed the intuitive sensitivity to distinguish between talk in terms of Zoku-tai and talk in terms of Shin-tai, he will, I am convinced, never get to the heart of the matter. My objection to many books on Buddhism by Westerners is that the authors have not, in my opinion, gotten the knack of threading their way through this tricky ground.

The contrast between the outward and ceremonial practices of Tōdai-ji and the subtleties of the *Kegon-kyō* upon whose teaching it is established is a good example of the way in which Zoku-tai and Shin-tai are interwoven in most forms of temple life in Japan. I am told it is the same, or more so, in other Mahayana lands.

• 20 •

UNIQUE in many ways, Rengeōin-ji's single building known as the Thirty-Three-Foundations-Hall (Sanjūsangen-dō) is so named for its exceptional length. In the center of its long, narrow main chamber, seated in meditation upon a raised dais, is an eight-foot-high image of Kannon, the Bodhisattva of Compassion. Extending forth in rows on both sides of this central figure like emanations of his thoughts are one thousand standing forms of Kannon each five feet seven inches tall. They are carved from wood, but are gilded to look as if they are solid gold. Each has several arms the hands of which hold various emblems of Compassion. On a series of ascending stages, one thousand mute shapes like so many living men stand side by side, all radiating a soft golden glow in the chamber's dim light. It is a fantastic sight!

Time and again I have heard newcomers give an involuntary gasp of amazement as they receive their first glimpse of this fabulous spectacle. From the walkway which runs the length of the room beside the bottom row of images the observer receives the impression of a veritable cloud of luminous beings floating before his eyes; he beholds a golden mist of hands outstretched to do him good.

What he sees is, in fact, an artistic representation of the proposition, Only-Mind is everything and everything is Nothing. There are so many of the Kannon figures they give the viewer the sensation of their being infinite in number. They can be said to represent the entire pluralistic universe. They signify, in effect, that over all things is cast the mysterious luster of Enlightenment. There is nothing which does not reflect the golden glow of Only-Mind, for all things equally are its manifestations. Caught up in the vision of the Sanjūsangen-dō, one feels that everything his glance falls upon is an occasion for the experience of the Compassion which the myriad Kannon images represent. I have explained that Mu-en-no-Jihi is impartial acceptance of everything in its As-is-ness. Entering the Mind-state of the central Bodhisattva seated there in meditation, the visitor to this exotic temple chamber perceives Kannon here, Kannon there, Kannon everywhere; whichever way he turns, Kannon, and again, Kannon. In short, he looks upon what might be called a "materialization" of the idea of Compassion.

Having walked the length of the hall and made the turn which leads behind the wall which forms the backdrop for the spectacle just described, the observer finds a much narrower corridor in which stand twenty-eight shapes quite different from those of Kannon. They are not Bodhisattvas; they are not golden. They are, instead, this-worldly persons of many different types: some warlike, some tranquil; some ugly, some beautiful; some wasted with starvation, some plump with prosperity. The significance of this array of individuals in varying conditions of life who stand just behind the multitude of Kannon forms is crystal clear. The golden tranquility of the universe of Compassion and the dark tensions which haunt the universe of diversity are but two sides of a single coin. Here is a visualization of the dialectic of the Middle-Way: simultaneous detachment and involvement, the One in the many and the many in the One. There are Not-Two; there is Not-One.

I recommend most highly a trip to Kyoto's Sanjūsan-gendō. In contrast to the stark plainness of a Zen-dō, it is garish and gaudy. It is the ebullient side of Mahayana, that side which states its position by means of accommodated language and deliberate myth (Hō-ben). The atmosphere of this type of Mahayana is in such sharp contrast to that of Zen, some might think it and Zen are totally different. In fact, each is a finger pointing to the same Moon of truth.

• 21 •

R. H. BLYTH dedicates his English translation of the *Mu-Mon Kan* "To Suzuki Daisetz, the Greatest Japanese of This Century." Many would agree. The present widespread interest in Zen in the Western world is chiefly the work of this one man. With freedom in the use of Chinese, Sanskrit, English, and his own native Japanese, this Zen Buddhist priest has been able to make available in English both important Indian sutras and also the writings of Chinese and Japanese Zenists of many centuries. These translations along with his own commentaries and his firsthand descriptions of Zen practice in the temples of modern Japan have won him world acclaim. His lectures in such noted halls of learning as Columbia University in New York have brought him into personal contact with many of the most influential thinkers of our day. I suspect that almost every Occidental presently writing in the field of Zen would state that it was through contact either with Suzuki's writings or with the man himself that his interest in this subject was kindled. Few missionaries have had the opportunity almost single-handedly to bring their faith to the notice of whole continents as Suzuki during his long life was able to do.

I began reading his books while still a seminary undergraduate. Later, after coming to Japan, I wrote to him from time to time and always received prompt and helpful replies. When I finally asked for the privilege of an interview at his residence in Kamakura's Engaku-ji, he sent a cordial invitation. That first visit was, as you can imagine, quite an unforgettable one for me. He was well advanced in years, very slight of stature, but the eyes beneath his bushy, white brows fairly crackled with genial intelligence. He put me at ease the first moment with his friendly, informal manner. His secretary, a beautiful American-born Japanese woman, graciously brought us tea. Then we began to talk, talked for some two hours. As usual, I had brought my small tape recorder and received his permission to use it. Later when I got back to Kyoto I made a copy of the tape and sent it to him. After Suzuki's death the Eastern Buddhist Society, with headquarters in Kyoto's Otani University, published a transcript of the interview in its quarterly, *The Eastern Buddhist*.[1] Of course the printed page cannot reproduce the

[1] *The Eastern Buddhist*, New Series, Vol. III, No. 1 (June 1970), pp. 108–21. To make clear my own particular method of conducting such

nuances of voice, the facial expressions, the gestures of the hands, but the words are all there.

We met on other occasions after that first interview. I attended a series of lectures he delivered at Jōdo-Shin-Shū's Otani University in Kyoto, and afterward received an invitation to visit him at his suite in the Miyako Hotel of that city. On his return to his Kamakura temple, he sent me a copy of his great translation of the *Lankavatara Sutra*, and also his definitive commentary on that sutra.[2] Such generosity was typical of the man. His personal magnetism is one of the factors which explain his wide influence as a teacher.

As an illustration of Suzuki's way of responding to questions and also as a sample of the sort of interview I have been conducting with Buddhist priests and teachers over the years, I include here that first conversation in Kamakura. Playing the tape takes me back to it all. Suzuki lives again in his voice:

*

---

interviews, I wish to state that my questions and comments were for the purpose of bringing forth statements which would make explicit my companion's views. In most cases I had already achieved what I believed to be satisfactory answers to the questions I raised, but I wanted to hear how the individual with whom I was in conversation would deal with them. Furthermore, I scrupulously avoided making what might appear to be dogmatic assertions about either Buddhism or Christianity. At no time did I attempt to argue a point. My whole approach was to put my Buddhist friend at ease and encourage him to speak his mind freely.

[2]Daisetz Teitaro Suzuki, *The Lankavatara Sutra, A Mahayana Text, Translated for the First Time from the Original Sanskrit* (London: George Routledge and Sons, Ltd., 1932), 300 pages.

Daisetz Teitaro Suzuki, *Studies in the Lankavatara Sutra, One of the Most Important Texts of Mahayana Buddhism, In Which Almost All Its Principal Tenets are Presented, Including the Teaching of Zen* (London: George Routledge and Sons, Ltd., 1930), 464 pages.

CALLAWAY: The question of the relationship between subject and object, the matter of experiencing the external world, the so-called external world within one's heart, please speak to me of such things.

SUZUKI: Well, my view is this. Western people start with the dualistic view of thinking, but Eastern people go further back. Further back means not in the chronological sense, but before we think, before we divide ourselves. There must be something which has not yet been divided. That is to say, before God said "Let there be light!" what did God have in his mind? Now, we want to start with that. Western people start with things after light separated itself from darkness. This is the great difference between the Eastern and Western minds. And then, by East and West, I don't mean the geographical division but the types of mind.

CALLAWAY: If I hold this teacup, it is my Western temptation to think that I am here and the teacup is over there. Please speak to me of the Zen attitude.

SUZUKI: The Zen attitude is before I hold this teacup, who is that who says, "I hold"? When you say "I" and the "teacup," they are already separated. The Eastern mind wants to know what is that "I" when you say "I hold teacup." Who makes you say "I"?

CALLAWAY: Can you say then that there is no "I" and no "teacup"?

SUZUKI: That's already "teacup" and "I". When "I" is not divided into "I" and "not-I," you may think that we can't say anything more. Yet, we can say something because we are born to say something.

CALLAWAY: So we are limited to the necessity of speech?

SUZUKI: Yes.

CALLAWAY: Therefore, what can we say regarding this?

SUZUKI: Well, we don't say anything.

CALLAWAY: Then we must be silent.

SUZUKI: Well, Buddha raised a bunch of flowers before the congregation and he did not say anything. One of his disciples smiled. And Buddha said to him, "I hand you the absolute mind-seal." Then you may ask, "When there is nothing to speak about, what mind-seal is there to be handed from one to another?" Really, there is no seal whatever.

CALLAWAY: I am seeking to understand the experience itself. I am not interested in the words. I wish to know the experience itself—the experience of the cup. There is the experience of the cup. We do not say the "I" and the "cup," but there is the cup, or there is the experience of the cup. There is the brightness, the wonder, the fullness of the being of the cup.

SUZUKI: Another way of saying what I have been saying is this. When you say, "I see the cup," there are the various senses at work—the senses of sight, touch, taste when you drink from it, and so on. These are all sensuous experiences. But what I speak of is before something is divided into the senses, five or six of them —Buddhists have six instead of five, the sixth corresponding to the intellect and not what the parapsychologists refer to as the sixth sense. Therefore, when you see the cup, instead of seeing the cup with the sense of sight, we see the cup with the sense of hearing. If we hear with the eye, and see with the ear, this is something of what I am trying to say, of not being divided into two, object and subject. There is something which sees with the ear and hears with the eye. That something we take hold of. Then we know the "I" before dividing itself into subject and object.

CALLAWAY: Is it the same being that hears the sound of one hand?

SUZUKI: Yes, you can say that. No sound comes out of one hand. Yet when you hear the sound, that sound we don't hear with the ear. You hear with the eye, or, it does not matter, you can say you hear with your touch. Seeing and hearing are senses more commonly experienced perhaps, so we generally say "to hear with the eye; to see with the ear." Daitō Kokushi, the founder of Daitokuji in Kyoto, once gave this statement to his disciples: "If your ears see, / And eyes hear, / Not a doubt you'll cherish / How naturally the rain drips / From the eaves!" So this "I" which is before I say "you" or "I" is nobody's "I." Some may call it "the universal I," Godhead, or absolute something before dividing into two. If you become that "I" you hear the sound coming out of one hand, and you know God before he said, "Let there be light!"

CALLAWAY: There must be deliverance from bondage to the belief in the objectivity of sensual experience.

SUZUKI: Yes, before you can say objectivity or subjectivity. There are existentialists nowadays who talk of death. Death, they say, is nothingness which overwhelmingly overtakes the philosopher, and they are afraid to taste it. But somehow it has to be tasted.

CALLAWAY: But if the person knows the universal self—may we use the word *mushin*—I know words are not adequate, but if we know the self before the senses, the *mushin*, the *muga*, then there is no birth, there is no death, and the concept of death becomes like other concepts. They are *kū*, they are *śūnyatā*. They have no self-existence, I think.

SUZUKI: That is right. That is a difficult point. When we

talk about *śūnyatā*, we think it is just sheer emptiness, and that emptiness is already standing in contrast to something which is not emptiness. But *śūnyatā* is absolute. It is beyond something and nothing, object and subject, birth and death, and so on. And yet, in that *śūnyatā* death takes place, birth takes place. That is why I say that it is something unlimited, absolute and infinite. Our lives are limited by things of finitude. Therefore we always feel dissatisfied. Rather, we might say that this very feeling of dissatisfaction comes from our wishing to go beyond, that is, to come to Godhead itself.

To put it another way, Godhead is beyond the reach of our senses, our intellect. Yet how is it that we have come to talk about it, to interview it, or come to identify with it? Of course, this idea of interviewing or identifying is already governed by our intellectual logic. So it is very difficult to express this in words, yet we have to use words. That is a contradiction, you might say. A dilemma is needed in which words at the same time ought to be all taken away in order to come to ultimate reality. But again if we think that ultimate reality stands outside ourselves, we miss the point. It is therefore not identifying in the sense of annihilation of all things. We are right in it, yet out of it. Zen people therefore say neither.

CALLAWAY: I believe you have been speaking in terms of what might be applied to the *chūdō* [the middle way] concept of there is neither existing nor not-existing. In one sense things exist. The cup is there, I see it. And yet in the other sense, it is not there, it has no objective being. Therefore, if we want the *chūdō* we say that the cup is and is not. Or neither is nor is not.

SUZUKI: And what Zen proposes is to realize that situation or position. As soon as we begin to talk we are so involved in contradictory terminology. A friend of mine, Kitarō Nishida, talks about the "identity of contradiction." And the Jōdo Shinshū people say "Namu-amida-butsu!" *Namu* is ourselves, and *amida-butsu* or Amida Buddha is over there. And they say *namu* and *amida-butsu* are one. But as soon as you say "they are one," you imagine one here and another one there and they become one with each other. This is not the way. Just "Namu-amida-butsu!" [Holding up the teacup . . .] So this is *namu-amida-butsu* drinking *namu-amida-butsu*. Yet we don't say that. When we say it, it is already wrong.

CALLAWAY: Then can we say that the *kansha*, the thanksgiving, of which the Jōdo Shin people speak is very similar to *jihi*, compassion, which we read in Zen? Is it a glad acceptance of all things as they are—can we say that?

SUZUKI: Shin people all want to go to the Pure Land. They are not satisfied with the *shaba* life. The *shaba* world is full of misery and sufferings. Psychologists these days might say fears, uncertainties, anxieties, and so on. But Shin people would say it is Amida who is making me feel this way so that we can go to him. It is Amida's summons, his calling to come to him, they say. That is to say Amida makes me feel uncertain about myself because the finite is always seeking after something infinite. The very word finite implies infinity. So when you ask a question, the answer is already in the question. When I am thankful to Amida, this feeling of thankfulness is Amida's gift, his favor.

CALLAWAY: I remember in one place, in one of your books,

you made the comment that perhaps there were more living cases of satori among the followers of Shin than within Zen circles. Say a little about that, please.

SUZUKI: That's what I think. They are called *Myōkōnin* and are wonderful individuals. Generally they are illiterate, not so learned as Zen people. Zen people are learned in classical Chinese and use it in their speech and writings very much. I think one of the finest examples of Myōkōnin is Shoma of Sanuki, who was a day laborer hired by people of his village to work in the paddy fields. One summer day, while working, perhaps weeding, he got so tired and, being hot, he came up to the temple porch and aired himself in the cool breeze. He felt so fine that he went into the temple and took Amida-san from the shrine, and binding him to the pole outside said, "Now you, too, cool yourself." That is very fine! He does not ask whether a wooden image has any feelings—that is not the point. He simply wants to share what he enjoys most with Amida, or with anybody in fact.

CALLAWAY: So it is this attitude, the attitude of gratitude or thankfulness which he feels though he cannot explain with words. He lives this gratitude.

SUZUKI: And that is what is called *jihi* [compassion]. Even an outlaw in case of a crisis forgets himself and jumps into the sea to help the baby from drowning. It is a strange thing. He may be notorious for his antisocial behavior usually, but when he sees a child in danger he jumps into the river at the risk of his own life. That kind of thing. Well, you may say that is instinct, but that instinct is something very good. You don't use your mind, no subjectivity, no objectivity, no sociality, nothing. He just jumps in. That act, thát feeling—absolute feeling, you might say—that is at the bottom of all our existence, we might say.

CALLAWAY: I think you use the term *hishiryo* [unthinkability].

SUZUKI: Yes.

CALLAWAY: Not thinking, but acting immediately or spontaneously.

SUZUKI: Yes, instantaneously. And that is what I'd like to talk to you about. You know Dr. Tillich?

CALLAWAY: Yes.

SUZUKI: Whenever we meet he talks so much about "participation," and I talk about "identity." And I say that participation cannot take place unless there is identity behind it. Unless you and that object are identical or share something there is nothing to respond to your participation. You cannot put anything of you into it.

CALLAWAY: Of course, at that point we Christians raise a question with you. We say, from our point of view, only if there is an objectively real person there over against this self, only if we have an objective relationship can we speak of love in the real sense. Love in the sense of giving oneself for another. We feel that objectivity or dualism is necessary.

SUZUKI: But before that dualism takes place, unless you and that object are identified, that participation, that feeling or sympathy, or compassion can't take place. Compassion already means we and what you call object are one.

CALLAWAY: We are speaking of Shin or Shinshū, and they make much use of the concept of *tariki* [other-power], of course, through the *hongan* (Original Vow), the power of *ganriki* [vow-power]. They receive salvation from the other [*ta*], and yet in the ultimate sense can we say there is a *ta*, a *tariki* [the other, the other-power]?

SUZUKI: This is another point. There is another Myōkōnin, Shin devotee, who died about thirty years ago, who used to say, "In *tariki* / There is neither / *jiriki* nor *tariki*." Now you see when you say *tariki*, *ta* [other] already involves *ji* [self], but Saichi does not bother about this at all. He simply says, "There is neither / *jiriki* nor *tariki*." And then, "*Tariki* all over, nothing but *tariki*! / Namu-amida-butsu / Namu-amida-butsu!" That "Namu-amida-butsu" is neither *tariki* nor *jiriki* [self-power]. It's absolute *tariki*.

CALLAWAY: So it would seem to me also that if we speak of *jiriki*, *tariki*, then we have "self," "other" and we have fallen into dualism.

SUZUKI: So it's simply "Namu-amida-butsu," or *tariki*, we say. This is where some people say Buddhism is pantheistic. But that is also wrong. *Ji* and *ta* are there, and yet with these it's all *ta*.

CALLAWAY: *Ji* and *ta* are there and yet it is all *ta*.

SUZUKI: Yes.

CALLAWAY: Or we can say it is all *ji* [self].

SUZUKI: We can say that, but *ji* has a certain odium about it, so we try to avoid it.

CALLAWAY: Yes, I understand you. Typically, people think of Zen-shū as *jiriki* or self-effort. They think of sects like Jōdo Shin as the Way of Faith. Yet you have some times spoken of faith in Zen. What do you mean by faith in Zen?

SUZUKI: It might be better to say that realization is faith. When you speak of faith there is something outside of yourself in which you take faith But that faith could never have taken place in you unless that object of faith was already in you.

CALLAWAY: So it is not faith in something other, but it is just realization.

SUZUKI: Yes. So you can say that that object comes to me and becomes one with me, or it may be better to say I go into the object and become one with it.

CALLAWAY: So though the people of Jōdo-Shin say, "We have the Way of Faith, Zen has the Way of *jiriki* or self-help," actually we cannot make this distinction. Zen also is faith or just realization or acceptance.

SUZUKI: Yes.

CALLAWAY: We have the Indian expression, *tathatā*. *Śūnyatā* and *tathatā* [emptiness and suchness] are closely related. In Japanese we say *shinnyo*. And you have also translated *shinnyo* as *sonomama* or *arugamama*.

SUZUKI: When Moses asked for God's name on Mt. Sinai, God said, "I am that I am." I understand the Hebrew gives this in a different grammatical tense, but that does not matter. "I am that I am," that's enough. And this is *shinnyo*.

CALLAWAY: Can we say *sonomama de ii, yoroshii* [All is well just as things are]?

SUZUKI: Yes, *sonomama de yoroshii*.

CALLAWAY: But we must first have the faith or the realization.

SUZUKI: Yes, realization. Shin people talk about our being destined for hell whatever we may do, and there's no hope except to believe in Amida. But how are we to believe in Amida if we are all bound for hell anyway? One devotee said, "Well, if there's no help, let me go to hell." She made her decision—theologians talk very much about decision—and the very moment of her decision, hell vanished and the blooming lotus flower received her. In this connection I often think of the case of the religious in despair. Some years ago, a student threw himself off the Kegon Fall in Nikkō, and he left a note saying that everything was beyond his understanding and he couldn't bear it any more. I am quite sure the very moment his feet stepped off the ridge he must have had a realization. But too late. When Darwin had a fall all his past appeared to him like a dream. Modern philosophers don't risk themselves by plunging into the abyss. They just peer from above and regard how terrible it is. They need pushing from behind. One must lose the individual in the infinite to discover being, you might say.

CALLAWAY: That's right. Shin people say *ōchō*, "leaping." A sort of "side-way leap."

SUZUKI: "Side-ways" means a leap not on the same plane but onto the plane of infinity. They did not have enough words in those ancient days, perhaps. This kind of leap is needed.

CALLAWAY: And it is given. That is what the Shin people would say is the gift of Amida. It is given. A man cannot choose it.

SUZUKI: No, man cannot choose it because in deciding, if you have a choice you can't jump in. You hesitate and run back. It is not of your own energy or will, but somehow there is a way.

CALLAWAY: In the *Tannishō*, the author speaks of the effects of the past karma, the karma of past lives, but, of course, karma also is *hōben*, just a device. There are no past lives in the historical sense?

SUZUKI: Quite. Now this is the way. There is no time, no history whatever. It's the present moment. As to karma, my own existence so called, objectively or dualistically speaking, did not come about of my own strength. I am not here on my own account. My parents gave birth to this biological presence, and we can go one after another up our ancestral tree all the way to God. There is something which moved in God and produced me. I am related biologically to all these people, but at the same time, somehow, as Buddha says, "Above heaven and below heaven, I alone am the most honored one!" I am something quite independent with individual feelings—"I am that I am." Biologically or sociologically, perhaps, I can trace my heritage. But there is something aside from this biological lineage which makes this "I" quite independent of this fact. There is something coming more directly. This I feel. This is directly connected with God's "I am that I am." And yet, I am I and God is different from me. God is God. I am not God, God is God, I am I. That is the important part.

CALLAWAY: You can say this, that I am I and it is it, as though there were two?

SUZUKI: When you think, when you begin to talk . . .

CALLAWAY: I see, in speech and only in speech . . .

SUZUKI: Speech need not necessarily involve the other. I may talk to myself, then I divide. But before I talk, before I think. This therefore cannot be expressed beyond this state, you might say. But that is because we are human beings. A cat, for instance, is a cat, and a dog, a dog. A dog barks, "Bow-wow," but he does not think "I am barking," "I am a dog."

CALLAWAY: This is the spontaneity as we have in calligraphy, in the making of the beautiful characters, the *kanji*. The same sort of spontaneity coming immediately. We do not stop to think . . .

SUZUKI: Well, if you say so, yes. It's true.

CALLAWAY: The brush moves rapidly. We do not pause to erase or to change.

SUZUKI: If you try consciously to form a good character, you can never do that. Spontaneous creativity must be like a crow when he cries, "Kah! kah!" In this sense Eckhart is very great. A little flea when he is inspired is greater than angels, he says. An angel without God is smaller than the flea. The flea, if it can come to have this awareness that we all have or can have, then it, too, can become conscious of divine presence. But divine presence does not mean that God turns into myself. If I should say "I am God" it is sacrilegious. No, not that. I am I, God is God, and at the same time I am God, God is I. That is the most important part.

CALLAWAY: And yet in the other sense, the essential self is God, so I am not God, I am God. And we're back to *chūdō*. We read in some writings of the *ichi-nen sanzen* and speak of the enlightenment of a grain of dust.

SUZUKI: *Sanzen* stands for *sanzen-daisen-sekai*, or "this great world." And *ichi-nen* or *eka-kshana* means just a little moment, an instant not in time but in eternity. Kierkegaard also has this word, "the instant in eternity." So it's the whole world in an instant.

CALLAWAY: The whole universe in one-thought.

SUZUKI: One-thought not in ordinary thinking, but one-instant. It's Dewey, is it not, who first used the term "here-now"? That means space and time are one. So the whole world in a particle of dust.

CALLAWAY: We read in the ancient scriptures, Shakyamuni says, "I have saved myriads of beings and yet I have saved no beings." If one thinks there is some being to be saved he cannot be called a bodhisattva.

SUZUKI: Yes, bodhisattva. He is a kind of savior. Usually, we think that if one is saved and another is not, then something is left unsaved. But when one is saved, all is saved. To realize the truth of this, you must be saved yourself. Then you can say that.

CALLAWAY: I cannot say self but—there are no words . . . but when realization comes the realization includes the salvation of the teacup which is within the realization, i.e., this cup is realized, the cup is saved.

SUZUKI: Yes. So we have in the Noh chants that the banana plant can be saved. Snow, too. That is where Eastern thought is so different from the West.

CALLAWAY: Yes. We think of salvation as an act of will, a choice made by an individual, and you say that a grain of dust can be saved. This is ridiculous, we think, because a grain of dust is inanimate. But from the Buddhist point of view, the realization of the true nature of the grain of sand is the salvation of the grain of sand.

SUZUKI: In the same way, you have in the Bible that God takes care of plants though they may be thrown into the oven tomorrow or even two minutes later. God takes care of each flower, each blade of grass. Why should God be so concerned about such insignificant plants, you might say? Yet God takes care of them just as much as he does Solomon in his glory.

CALLAWAY: However when we Christians speak like this, we mean there is really a God and there are really plants apart from one another—as Creator and created things. But in Buddhism, I believe, we cannot speak of Creator and creation.

SUZUKI: So the Creator is the created, and yet the Creator is Creator. That's it. That must be emphasized.

CALLAWAY: Creation is the Creator, and the Creator is creation.

SUZUKI: So, it is constant, continuous creation.

SUZUKI: There is in Buddhism what is called *mu-en no jihi. En* is relation or causal relationship. Generally, we may have relationship with this and this person and we may have compassion [*jihi*] for those persons. But *mu-en* means no special relationship. No reward is expected, no return. It is compassion simply going out.

CALLAWAY: So Christian love would be *u-en no jihi* [relative compassion]?

SUZUKI: Christians speak about *agape* and *eros*. And God's love is *agape*. This is *mu-en no jihi*. Christians also have *u-en no jihi* and that is *eros*.

CALLAWAY: In other words, Christian love involves relationship and Buddhist love exists without relationship.

SUZUKI: Yes, when you are struck on the right cheek, then you turn your left cheek. But Buddhists wouldn't do that. Right cheek is struck, well, just stay there. Don't turn the left. This is where I object to the Christian idea. Because they talk about left and right.

CALLAWAY: Yes. It seems that Buddhism says *sonomama ga yoroshii*, but Christianity says *sonomama ga yokunai* (all is not well just as things are).

SUZUKI: Yes, more or less.

CALLAWAY: So we must try to improve things. We wish to change things.

SUZUKI: Yes, that's the good side of Christianity. Buddhists accept everything as it is, perhaps. That is bad. They don't go out of their way to do good.

CALLAWAY: That's the meaning of turning the other cheek, you see. We turn the other cheek to show our love for the enemy. It is to show love for the enemy. And if we do not turn the other cheek, he does not know our love.

SUZUKI: So, you see, Buddhism does not talk about enemy.

CALLAWAY: Yes. So there is no enemy.

SUZUKI: Buddhism does not say "love thine enemy" because there is no enemy.

CALLAWAY: That's true. And no "you" to have an enemy.

SUZUKI: That's *mu-en no jihi.*

CALLAWAY: That's a very good expression.

SUZUKI: So Buddhism has a great deal to learn from Christianity. Lately, I have been emphasizing what may be called "activism." Act is needed, work is needed.

• • •

After the interview I turned off the recorder. We drank more tea, he showed me some interesting objects of art in the cozy sitting room. We bid farewell Japanese style with mutual bows. I went away with impressions and memories I shall cherish always.

SECTION

III

ZEN WAY—JESUS WAY

22

MY LOVE for Japan was Jesus-born. In the fall of 1944, at the height of World War II, when hatred for the Japanese people was rampant and their very humanity was denied by many in the United States, the words of Christ, my Lord, struck home to me. "Love your enemies, pray for those who mistreat you"; "Do not resist one who is evil. . . .Go with him a second mile" (Matthew 5 : 44, 39, 41). Who more than the Japanese matched the description of those to whom Jesus would have me give myself. A graduate student in a theological seminary at the time, I forthwith applied to the foreign mission board of my denomination for assignment to Japan. A mark of the quality of the board's leadership was the fact that it appointed my wife and me to Japan in April 1945, while the war with that country was still fiercely raging.

When at last, in the summer of 1947, the Allied Occupation Forces opened the door of the country for civilians to enter, I went at once. Since wives and children were not yet permitted, I had to go alone, arriving in Yokohama on a converted troop carrier August 27, 1947. I was the first postwar appointee of my denomination to set foot on Japanese soil.

It is not my purpose to be autobiographical, but some understanding of my motivation, the depth of my sense of Christian vocation, should help the reader to see why I have sought with all my might to gain a sympathetic grasp of the Buddhist experience. Both my studies before arrival and my early years in Japan when I was engaged in learning her language and her ways led me to believe that the key to a genuine comprehension of the mind of the Japanese was an in-depth examination of her religions. Shintoism and Confucianism play a very important role and I have given much time to them, but it is my conviction that the mood and manner most characteristically "Japanese" is of Buddhist origin. The tea ceremony, the art of flower arrangement, garden design, judo, and most of those cultural phenomena associated by Westerners with what is most typically and uniquely Japanese are rooted in Buddhism.

Much more than they themselves are aware, I believe, the moods and attitudes of the people of Japan have about them the scent of the sutras. Not that the average Japanese today would claim to be familiar with the sort of Buddhist doctrine set forth in the two previous sections of this book. Few have ever read even one of the hundreds of Mahayana scriptures. Most limit their temple going to participation in memorial ceremonies for the dead, occasional visits to get the supernatural, good-luck-causing forces on their side, or to picnics in the lovely natural surroundings of the temple sites. Within the home, overt Buddhist activity usually is limited to acts of obeisance before the Butsu-dan (literally, "Buddha-Shelf") upon which are kept wooden plaques representing the presence of family members who have passed away. One interesting expression for saying very politely that someone has died is that he "*Hotoke ni narimashita*" (he "Buddha has become"). There is ordinarily no thought here that the individual who passed away had achieved Enlightenment in the profound sense I have been describing. It comes nearer meaning he has passed over into paradise. And it is more a courtesy phrase than a serious belief.

While the nominal nature of popular Buddhism in Japan can hardly be exaggerated, I am nevertheless convinced that in countless ways which these nominal Buddhists themselves do not suspect, their emotions and thoughts have the flavor of Buddhism. In much the same way, there are many Americans who never go to church except for weddings and have never read even one book of the Bible, whose moral judgments and general world-view are nevertheless influenced by Christian doctrine in ways they themselves fail to realize. They have been conditioned by a culture grounded in Biblical traditions. Any Oriental student of the American mind must go deeply into Christianity if he hopes to gain any meaningful knowledge of that mind. It early became apparent to me that if I were to have anything more than a superficial grasp of how a Japanese person thinks and feels, I had to know Buddhism and had to know it from the inside.

The language of Japan is largely Buddhist in essence. Her written language was introduced from China in the form of Buddhist sutras. Early scholarship in Japan was almost exclusively devoted to learning the Chinese ideographs in order to read those sutras. Our foreign mission board has the wise policy of requiring two years of full-time study of the language before its missionaries are allowed to undertake any other work. In order to understand the nuances of the Japanese words I was learning during such study, I found that a knowledge of their Buddhist implications was most helpful. When a Christian teacher or minister attempts to explain the meaning of his faith to Japanese hearers, he has to do this with a Buddhist vocabulary. At the beginning, he may be tempted to take the dictionary's English equivalent of the Japanese word he is learning to be the full meaning of that word. Thus he finds that the Japanese word for "compassion" is *jihi*, and assumes thenceforth that when he says *jihi* his Japanese hearer is thinking "compassion" in the Christian sense. I hope by now it is clear that "it ain't necessarily so!" Again and again I discovered that the Japanese expression I was using had its English meaning to me, but for my Japanese companions was cloaked with emotional and cognitive implications which had me perplexed. I thought I was speaking "Christian" Japanese; they were hearing "Buddhist" Japanese.

For such reasons, as my study of the language continued and my contact with the people became more intimate, I was more and more convinced that for Christ's sake I had to know Buddhism. The New Testament says of Jesus that "he himself knew what was in man" (John 2 : 25). It was clear to me that if I was to be Christ's man in Japan, I needed to know what was "in" the Japanese. And to a large extent, this was Buddhism.

• 23 •

OBVIOUSLY, mere reading would not be enough to gain the sort of understanding I wanted. My interest was not in terms and concepts as such, but in their experiential content. Japanese studies were beginning to open up the whole fascinating world of the Chinese-Japanese ideographs. The sutras in the form the Chinese and Japanese Buddhists read them were becoming more and more accessible to me, but in addition to this I wanted to find how No-thingness (Mu), Emptiness (Kū), Not-Two (Fu-ni), Only-Mind (Yui-shin), Nothing-Mind (Mu-shin), No-thing-Self (Mu-ga), and As-is-ness (Shin-nyo), for example, actually *felt* to a man who had committed his life to a belief in the sort of reality they imply.

For Jesus' sake, I was determined to enter into the very essence of the Buddhist experience. As already indicated, my work assignment as a missionary was to serve as professor of World Religions and Philosophy of Religion at Seinan Gakuin University in the city of Fukuoka. I used holiday periods for visiting well-known Buddhists and Buddhist temples up and down the land. Then, as mentioned in earlier chapters, I was given the privilege of living for five years in the chief center of Japanese Buddhism, the city of Kyoto. During this time I commuted regularly to my university in Fukuoka for lectures. Also, by the kindness of Dr. Masatoshi Doi, Professor of Theology at Doshisha University, and Director of the National Christian Council's Center for the Study of Japanese Religions in Kyoto, I was given the opportunity to lecture at Doshisha and to have the use of the library and other facilities at the NCC Center. Since for some twenty years I was many hours each week in Buddhist temples talking with their residents and observing their practices, I in fact spent much more time there than in Christian churches.

But this I did for Christ.

My approach was always basically the same. I would introduce myself as a Christian who because of Christ loved Japan and wished to understand her people. I would state my conviction that only through understanding Buddhism could I achieve that objective, and then would ask for help in that direction. In more than two hundred contacts made in such a way, I was never a single time rebuffed, but invariably received the sort of interested, often enthusiastic, always gracious reception already illustrated. Often I was invited to return again and again for continuing dialogue.

And most of these sustained interviews became a dialogue in the truest sense. Although we would begin with my questions about Buddhism, before we were finished the monk or priest would almost invariably start asking me what Christians felt and believed about the matters we had been discussing from a Buddhist point of view. In not a few cases, it turned out I was the first Christian with whom my Buddhist companion had ever spoken seriously. Although it was not conventional evangelism, I nevertheless felt that I was responding to a special command from Christ to help these deeply committed Buddhist friends get a more meaningful understanding of what Christians believe. I found that many of their notions about those beliefs were almost as sketchy and incomplete as the average Christians' understanding of Buddhist beliefs would have been.

My interest in what these men had to say and my affection for them as persons were not feigned. As the Apostle Paul felt a particular love for the gentiles to whom he believed Jesus had appointed him a witness, so did I for Japanese Buddhist leaders. This present book is in part a fulfillment of what I believe to be a Christ-inspired mission to all who are earnestly seeking to walk the Middle-Way. I hope many of those who helped me in my understanding of Buddhism will read it and be led to a more complete understanding of the way of Jesus.

What I wish to do in the following pages is to set the Zen Way and the Jesus Way side by side in order to show what each has to say about the fundamental issues of human life. It should already be apparent to anyone who has come this far with me that he must do away with the sort of tepid sentimentality which feels it is unfriendly to believe that different religions are truly different. The old simile that the various faiths are like separate roads leading to the peak of the same mountain is pleasing to our sense of goodwill toward all men. If, however, one goes beyond mere sentiment to a genuine concern to know what religions believe about the nature of ultimate reality, one finds elemental differences. Even as my Buddhist companion of the hour and I respected each other—even as I "loved" him and he felt "Compassion" toward me—one point was always made penetratingly obvious as we went along. On the level of basic presuppositions, interpretation of experience, and resulting life-style, the way of Zen and the way of Jesus are separated by an unbridgeable gulf. The differences are not just a matter of semantics, but concern the very root and substance of the two.

All men share essentially the same human nature. Their needs on all levels are very similar. All religions attempt to answer the same fundamental questions regarding the character of ultimate reality, the nature and destiny of man, the most satisfactory way to relate to other persons, how to cope with the sufferings and frustrations of life. Although religions are much alike in the problems they pose, they divide in the solutions they offer.

A good example of the radical cleavage between the Zen Way and the Jesus Way is their respective answers to the question of the proper relationship between religions. Each advocates "tolerance" and denounces "intolerance," but each means something quite different by these terms.

For Zen, "tolerance" means believing everything is Only-Mind and, therefore, is good just as it is. The doctrines and beliefs of all religions, as well as the emotional experiences upon which they are grounded, are all dreams created on the Sixth Level of the Eight-Consciousnesses. This is true of all intellectual and emotional activities. No religion or philosophy or system of thought or doctrinal structure is either true or false. I have repeatedly emphasized that the hallmark of Enlightenment is the realization that every value judgment is meaningless. All which can be said of any particular thought is simply that Only-Mind is dreaming it. From the standpoint of Satori, Jesus, his way, all Christian believers, the Bible, all the books which have been written on Christian subjects, all sermons, all churches, all Christian theology—like everything else—*are* the Buddha-Mind. Jesus *is* Buddha, just as all things *are* Buddha. There is nothing which is not the Buddha-Mind. This realization is what Zen means by "tolerance." This "tolerance" is the same as Zen Compassion. If it be seriously believed that any one thing is more true or better than any other thing, Zen would say such a belief is the mark of Ignorance (Mu-myō).

It follows that the Christian conviction that Jesus is the uniquely perfect window into the heart of reality and therefore the standard by which everything must be judged, is the depth of darkness to the eyes of Zen. In fact, Zen cannot even believe that Zen's own doctrine is more true than the doctrine of other religions. The moment one thing is preferred to another, the realization that all things are equally Only-Mind has been set aside. This leads to the basic dilemma of Zen and, for that matter, of all other monistic or nondualistic systems of thought. The only possible conclusion to believing that the insights of Zen are true is to believe that truth cannot be known. But if it is believed that truth cannot be known, it cannot be believed that the premises of Zen are true. In a word, to think Zen is true means to think Zen is not true. In actual practice, Enlightened Zenists do believe in the truth of the Zen presuppositions: I am Only-Mind; Only-Mind is everything; everything is No-thing. To restate the Zen position on religious tolerance in these terms, make a mathematical formula such as the following and let "*x*" be any religion, any theological system, any philosophical position you choose:

x = Only-Mind = I = Buddha-Mind =
each thing = No-thing

Any portion of this formula is wholly interchangeable with any other portion. Let x be Jesus, and see what you have; let x be the New Testament, and see what you have; let x be Zen, or Gautama Buddha, or the *Hannya-Shin-gyō*, and see what you have; let x be Marxism, or Islam, or Methodist doctrine, and see what you have!

In a word, the "tolerance" of Zen, and of all monistic or nondualistic religions, is the acceptance of *the absolute qualitative identity* of all things, including all religions. If this position is seriously held to be true, the claim of Jesus to be "*the* way, *the* truth, and *the* life" (John 14 : 6) is manifestly false. Zenists commit their very lives to a belief in this absolute qualitative identity. This is the cornerstone of Zen dogma. I heard one say, "The only thing I cannot tolerate is intolerance!" As he continued to speak it became evident that by "intolerance" he meant the belief that one system of thought is more true than another. He was actually saying that he could only tolerate those who agreed with him in his belief concerning the nature of ultimate reality. He had an absolute belief in the relativity of truth and claimed to be intolerant of anyone who did not share this conviction. It is ironic that those committed to absolute tolerance sometimes affirm it with intolerant dogmatism.

What I as a Christian mean by "tolerance" is demonstrated by more than half a lifetime spent in showing the respect I genuinely feel for Buddhists whose basic beliefs are to me completely false. Furthermore, motivated by what I take to be Jesus-inspired goodwill, I have made an earnest effort to gain an objectively accurate understanding of those beliefs so contrary to my own. In my view, the elements of true tolerance are respect for the man whose beliefs I do not share and the wish to gain an accurate understanding of his beliefs.

The Zenist who is faithful to the Understanding to which he awakened in his experience of Enlightenment *must*, on his presuppositions, deny the claim of any religious leader to offer a more perfect revelation of reality than another. He *must* assert the absolute, qualitative identity of all those leaders.

On the other hand, the Christian who has devoted his life to a belief in Jesus' affirmation, "He who has seen me has seen the Father" (John 14 : 9), *must*, on his presuppositions assert that the most perfect revelation of the nature of ultimate reality is the personal character of this same Jesus. He *must* deny all systems of experience and thought whose presuppositions leave no room for this kind of absolute value judgment.

Here at the outset of Section III, it is already apparent that on the level of their basic assumptions the way of Zen and the way of Jesus do not meet. It is no good for a Jesus person to rail at the Zen Buddhist for what—from his Christian standpoint—is an amorphous, frustratingly intangible, and insubstantial relativism which dogmatically insists that all religions are the same.

It is no good for the Zenist to be revolted at the follower of Jesus for what—from his Buddhist viewpoint—is the Christian's benighted attachment to one way as if it were qualitatively much better than all the others.

We won't get anywhere browbeating one another for doing and thinking exactly what the presuppositions of our respective religions require of us.

Shall we ever get anywhere by practicing the sort of intolerance which says, "I can tolerate everyone except those who disagree with my fundamental assumptions?"

I venture to say that the most fruitful and enriching approach is for the adherents of both the Zen Way and the Jesus Way to make an earnest and sympathetic effort to understand the heart of what the other believes. If each has a clear grasp of the rock-bottom premises of the other's Way, then in a spirit of mutual respect, the Zen-man and the Jesus-man can talk together. More than this, for the first time they will be in a position to make a meaningful comparison and contrast of their own faith with that of the other. Instead of hurling scornful condemnations at each other for not conforming to the implications of each other's basic assumptions, both the Zenist and the Christian can find how fully each is fulfilling the implications of his own chosen faith. And upon gaining such an understanding, each will be in a position to see if he is satisfied with the particular presuppositions upon which he has chosen to build his life.

From this you can see why I prefer to talk to an informed and deeply consecrated Buddhist instead of a merely nominal and indifferent one. It is as I encounter a man who knows what he believes and has dared to risk his whole life on this belief that a genuine dialogue is possible. I'm smiling as I write. I am remembering how often a Zen friend and I have done this very sort of thing; and as with Christian love I have addressed him as a genuine other, I have understood well that to him both he and I were Not-Two, but were Only-Mind.

• 24 •

OVER AGAINST the Nondualistic Idealism or Monistic Idealism of Zen, the Jesus Way is grounded in what I am calling Pluralistic Materialism. While the basic presupposition of Zen is "I, Only-Mind, am everything, and everything is No-thing but my thought," a fundamental premise of the Jesus Way is "The Creator is other than his creations; I am one creature among many, and everything is one creature among many."

From a different point of view, the Jesus Way is a modified Dualism. The Creator is ultimate reality; his creations are derived reality. This dualism is "modified" in the sense that while the Creator is essentially *other* than creation, he is also *in* it as the continuing source of its existence and the director of its development in the direction of his creative purposes. In more technical theological terms the Creator is

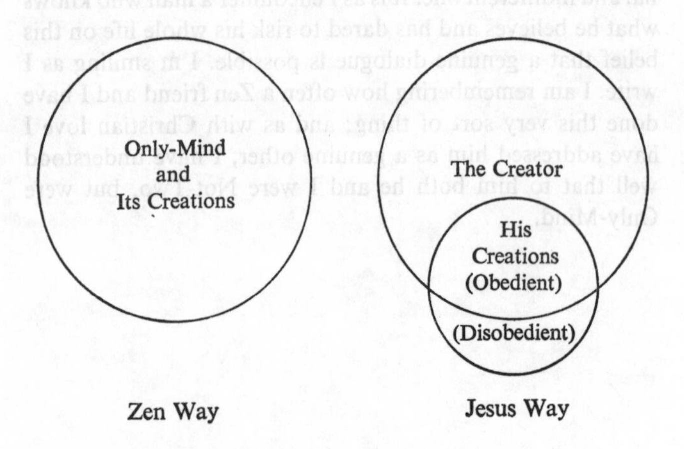

both Transcendent to and Immanent in his creation. While Zen Enlightenment can depict Only-Mind and its creations as a single circle, Christians can picture the Creator and his Creations as two partially overlapping circles, one large and one small.

A great portion of creation is within the Creator's *purposive will*; there is also a portion of creation outside his purposive will, but this is there in accordance with his *permissive will*. The Creator in his own nature is vastly more than can be expressed in his creations. If you look again at the figure with the partially overlapping circles, you will see that it suggests these various aspects of the relationship.

According to Christian belief, the connection between the human creature and his Creator is unique. All nonhuman creatures perfectly obey the Creator's will because they have no self-determination. Nonhuman creatures, therefore, have no moral responsibility, are incapable of doing either "good" or "evil." They are like puppets; they move only as the Creator pulls the strings. No creature "sins" but man. Human creatures alone have been given self-determination or freedom of will. When the Bible says man was made in the image of his Creator, it is this innate capacity for independent, self-conscious, purposeful thought and action which is indicated. I was interested to find that some Buddhists took this Biblical teaching to mean Christians believe the Creator had a man-shaped body. Let me nail this down at once! The Bible says the Creator is Spirit, equally present in all portions of the universe at once. Obviously, all anthropomorphism is childish imagery. The Bible indicates that the "form" and "substance" of the Creator are absolutely ineffable.

In contrast to Zen, for which all thoughts and all individual minds are the Only-Mind, the Bible depicts the ultimate thoughts of the Creator to be far beyond the capacity of created human minds to comprehend:

> My thoughts are not your thoughts,
> Neither are your ways my ways,
> says the Lord.
> For as the heavens are higher than the earth,
> So are my ways higher than your ways,
> And my thoughts higher than your thoughts.
> (Isaiah 55 : 8f.)

In such passages, genuine separation between the mind of the Creator and the minds of human creatures is clearly affirmed.

Let me assure my Buddhist readers that to be a Christian does not require one to believe in a God who is like an old man with a white beard who flies through the sky on feathered wings. On the contrary, the Christian scriptures present the concept of a Creator whose form and whose mind are transcendent to his creation. In my diagram above, the area of the Creator's transcendence above and beyond the ken of human understanding is suggested by the portion of the larger circle which is outside the smaller one.

As a Jesus-man, I have no idea of the form of the Creator. When I read in the Bible that I am made in his image, to me this means that I have been given self-determination, the freedom to choose a particular goal and move toward it; that within the arena of creation, and with the Creator's guidance, I myself can be a creator.

The self-determination of the human creature brings him into confrontation with his Creator in what philosopher Martin Buber called an "I-Thou" relationship. Creator and creature meet in a subject-subject encounter. In this encounter they are two separate Egos in dialogue. According to the Christian view, this I-Thou relationship, in which each individual is free either to give or to withhold himself, is just as possible between each human creature and his Creator as it is between each human creature and every other human creature. Human creatures can also relate to each animal, vegetable, and mineral creature in proportion to that creature's capacity to respond to, or to be molded by them.

How different from the world of Zen is the one I have just been describing! Where Zen would say, "Not-Two," Jesus says, "Two"; where Zen would say, "No-thing-Self," Jesus says, "Countless individual, self-determining selves"; where Zen would say, "Only-Mind," Jesus says, "The mind of the Creator and the minds of his human creatures in genuine dialogue"; where Zen would say, "Everything, just as it is, is good," Jesus says, "Everything which is done in defiance of the Creator's will is not good." The world of Zen is a non-material, dimensionless dream of Only-Mind; the world of Jesus is composed of material entities in three-dimensional space and linear time which constitutes an environment for deliberate human activity either in obedience or in disobedience to the Creator's will.

• 25 •

BUT I MUST go further than this. It is necessary to look at the very heart of the distinctively Christian teaching about the relationship between the Creator and his human creatures. In theological terms, it is called the doctrine of Original Sin. The Bible says that long ago man exercised his freedom of self-determination to violate his Creator's intention for his life. Instead of living in childlike obedience to the leadership of his Heavenly Father, man resolved to be his own master. Man was made to be the dwelling place for the Creator's Love-Spirit. Instead, he became agressively egocentric, attempting to gratify his own desires at the expense of others. The distortions of human nature which resulted have been inherited by all subsequent generations. Christians believe men are born with the inclination to rebel against their true reason for being.

Although this is in contradiction to the Creator's purposive will, it is in accord with his permissive will. He desires to lead men into the joy of self-forgetting Love; for this very reason, he permits them the liberty to renounce that joy.

If Jesus was right, man was made for Love. The essence of Love is free choice. Love is a meaningful and responsible motive only if selfish indifference is equally possible. A puppet can neither love nor hate; man can do each because he is free to do the other.

In the original Greek New Testament, the most frequently used word for "sin" was *hamartia*, meaning "to miss a target." It was a military term having to do with archery. When an arrow flew wide of its mark, that was *hamartia*. When a Christian speaks of "sin," he means "missing the target" for which man was made, namely, to live his life in voluntary slavery to the Creator's Love-Spirit. The New Testament says, "All have missed the mark" (Romans 3 : 23).

To an Enlightened Zenist, the concept of separate Egos each free either to obey or to disobey the will of his Creator is manifest nonsense. There is Only-Mind; individual selves exist as its dreams. All the activities of a particular dream-image are nothing but the projections of the Mind which dreams them. The image cannot act on its own as if it were an independent entity.

The tranquility which Zen gives rests upon the realization that there is no responsibility to pursue what is "good" and to flee what is "evil." The essence of Zen peace is the glad acceptance of everything just as it is. If a Zen-man should seriously allow himself to believe he could "miss the target" toward which Only-Mind aimed him, he would quickly find himself back in that world of conflicts and tensions from which Satori had liberated him. He would have to believe once again in real individual selfhood, in real otherness, in real choices between real alternatives. He would be plunged once more into the darkness of Ignorance.

Sin is unthinkable. Compassion welcomes every type of person and every form of conduct as being the Buddha-Mind itself. Everything in its As-is-ness is good.

Notice that in this typical Zen assertion, "good" is not a comparative evaluation. It does not distinguish some things from other things which are "not good." It does not describe anything. In this sense, "good" is simply another appellation for Only-Mind. To say, "Everything is good," and to say, "Everything is Only-Mind," is to repeat oneself. If all were light, the word "light" would lose its qualifying significance. "Light" is descriptive only when it designates a condition which is in contrast to "darkness."

For Zen, there is no sin.

For Jesus, all have sinned.

• 26 •

THIS BRINGS me to an even more definitive presupposition of the Jesus Way. Most of the assertions made above are equally shared with Jewish friends whose understanding of the character of the Creator includes all the Old Testament, but excludes the New Testament. That particular belief or fundamental assumption which sets the Jesus Way most completely apart from every other way is forcefully stated in John 14 : 9, where Jesus says simply, "He who has seen me has seen the Father." By "the Father" he means "the Creator." Jesus is saying, if you want to know the true character of the Creator, see what sort of person I am. Jesus is saying men can know the true nature of ultimate reality so far as human beings are concerned by observing his way of life. By coming to know him, by coming to understand his thoughts, his feelings, his mind, his heart, one gains knowledge of the mind of the Creator himself.

John says the same thing in his gospel: "No one has ever seen God; the only Son . . . has made him known" (John 1: 18). Some non-Christians are repelled by the New Testament teaching that Jesus is the "only Son" of the Father-Creator, feeling that it introduces sexuality into the concept of Deity. In the New Testament, the primary significance of the Father-Son relationship between Jesus and the Creator is the likeness between them. This is the sort of likeness expressed in the common idiom, "He is a true son of his father"; or, "This boy is no longer a son of mine!" The "true son" walks in his father's footsteps, is committed to the same ideals, is obedient to things he has learned from his father. In the second expression, the father is not questioning the biological legitimacy of his son; he is disowning him because of blatant disobedience to his parental instructions. The New Testament says of Jesus' mother, Mary, that the child was conceived in her "by the Holy Spirit" (Matthew 1 : 20). Whatever else this may mean, it clearly signifies that Jesus was born of, and therefore indwelt by, the Creator's Love-Spirit. It follows that his whole life was a revelation of the Spirit or Character of the Creator. This is the germinal idea in the New Testament affirmation that Jesus is "the only begotten Son of God" (John 3 : 16). The manner of the Conception of Jesus is a mystery; in no sense does it imply sexual intercourse between an earthly woman and a supernatural Man!

The first chapter of John clearly points up the salient elements in the doctrine that Jesus is uniquely the Son of God:

> Before the world was created, the Word already existed.
> . . . not one thing in all creation was made without him.
> . . . The Word became a human being and lived among us.
> . . . No one has ever seen God. The only One, who is the same as God and is at the Father's side, he has made him known. (John 1 : 1–18 TEV)[1]

The agent in creation is the Creator's Word. A "word" is a tangible expression of a thought. All creation, therefore, is a tangible expression of the Mind of the Creator, his Word. But—and this is the crucial point for Jesus-people—once and only once in human history, the Creator's Word became a perfect human being. As a person's true words

[1]TEV = Today's English Version (*Good News for Modern Man*).

articulate his thoughts and feelings, so Jesus, the Creator's Word who had become a man, articulated the thoughts and feelings of the Creator. Accordingly, he alone is able to make the Creator known in an absolute manner. To say that Jesus was born of the Creator's Holy Spirit or to say Jesus was the Creator's Word who had become a man of flesh and blood is to say the same thing two different ways.

The Apostle Paul puts it thus: "Christ is the visible likeness of the invisible God. He is the first-born Son, superior to all created things. For by him God created everything in heaven and on earth" (Colossians 1 : 15f. TEV). Another translation has "He is the image of the invisible God" (RSV).[2] Elsewhere Paul writes of "Christ, who is the exact likeness of God" (2 Corinthians 4 : 4 TEV). The author of Hebrews says:

> In many and various ways God spoke of old to our fathers by the prophets; but in these last days he has spoken to us by a Son, whom he appointed the heir of all things, through whom he created the world. This Son reflects the light of the Creator's truth and bears the very stamp of his nature. . . .
>
> (Hebrews 1 : 1–3 RSV, altered)

There are many other passages from the New Testament which repeat this same idea; namely, that in the human being Jesus we have an absolute revelation of the character of ultimate reality. He is the visible likeness of the invisible Creator—his exact likeness. To see him is to see the Creator. He, Jesus, bears the very stamp of the Creator's nature.

What I want my Buddhist friends and all readers of this

[2]RSV = Revised Standard Version.

book to see is that to be a Christian means above all else to believe that in Jesus men have a unique and perfect and absolute revelation of the distinctive quality of essential being.

Please do not misunderstand me. I am by no means saying I believe that I or any other follower of Jesus has a perfect knowledge of absolute truth! If you will reread the above you will find I am saying something quite different. I am saying we Christians believe that absolute and perfect truth about the nature of ultimate reality is shown *in Jesus*. All the Christians I have ever met, or read about, begin by confessing that their understanding of the Truth which Jesus *is* is very limited and imperfect and that their ability to live in accordance with what they understand is even more limited and imperfect. This brings me back to the subject of man's created capacity to "miss the target," to "sin."

We Christians believe all men including ourselves are sinners. In fact, we believe that only as a man comes to know Jesus can he realize what it means to be a sinner. Jesus' Way is the "target" we are supposed to hit. A man can come to know what he is, and what he is not, as he measures himself by the perfect man, Jesus. If Jesus is the revelation of the true nature of reality, this means he embodies ideal human nature. As the Creator's living Word, he expresses the purposes for which all human beings were made. In revealing the perfect image of what a man was created to be, he becomes a model or example. In the words of Peter, "Christ suffered for you, leaving you an example, that you should follow in his steps. He committed no sin" (1 Peter 2 : 21f.).

Peter's assertion that Jesus "committed no sin" is another way of saying he was the flawless expression of the nature of the Creator. If he did not sin, he obeyed the Mind of the

Maker in all things; therefore, his life is a perfect manifestation of the Maker's basic intentions for every human creature. Jesus was sinless; what he was in himself is the "target" which to miss is sin.

• 27 •

IT CAN readily be seen that belief in Jesus as the only perfect revelation of the nature of the Creator is not peripheral and arbitrary, but the very keystone of the whole system of Christian thought. When fully understood, this belief is the single most definitive presupposition of Christian theology. Everything else follows from it.

Since sin is a departure from the Way of Jesus, salvation from sin must be a return to that Way. To be saved from sin means finally to be brought into perfect obedience to the Creator's will as Jesus was perfectly obedient. The ultimate expectation of every Jesus-man is to be re-created into the exact likeness of his Lord.

Now I cannot believe any reader will be so literalistic as to think I am talking about physical likeness. It does not mean that as a Christian I should wear a long, white robe and go about in a style appropriate to first century Palestine. It means, rather, that through deliberately opening myself to the Creator's Love-Spirit, I will be remade to conform to the character of Jesus. When the salvation process is completed I shall have become precisely that particular individual the Creator originally intended me to be. To be like Jesus does not mean going through exactly the same experiences in exactly the same way he did. It means to be totally in harmony with the Creator's will: doing in my time and place with my own distinctive abilities just what I was created to do.

When, as a Christian, I speak of "faith" or "belief" or "trust," I most emphatically do not mean accepting something as true in spite of all evidence to the contrary. What I mean by these terms is an attitude of willingness to let myself be changed into the likeness of Jesus. Faith is saying "Yes" to the elemental forces of reality. Trust is saying to the Creator, "Do your thing in me!" Belief is betting my life that Jesus is "THE way, THE truth, THE life."

If I fly from San Francisco to Tokyo by Japan Air Lines, entering the plane is an act of "faith"; coming off the plane in Tokyo is an act of "knowledge." When I get aboard, I "believe" Japan Air Lines has supplied a safe plane, a competent pilot, and will take me to the destination marked on the ticket; when I walk down the steps and find myself in Tokyo's Haneda Airport, I "know" those things I have "believed" are so. This is what I mean when I say I have faith in Jesus. I believe that if I submit myself to the creative powers of ultimate reality revealed in his life, I will be remade into his likeness. This is precisely what the New Testament promises:

> We all, with unveiled face, beholding the light of the Lord, are being changed into his likeness from one degree of brightness to another; for this comes from the Lord who is the Spirit. (2 Corinthians 3 : 18)

As I let myself down upon the elemental realities of the Creator—reconciled to him after long estrangement—he, the Lord who is the Spirit, commences in me the saving process by which I am gradually and inexorably transformed into the likeness of Jesus.

Paul writes, "If anyone is in Christ, he is a new creation; the old has passed away, behold, the new has come" (2 Corinthians 5 : 17). To be "in Christ" is to be united with him in one's inmost being. The same Holy Spirit by whom he was conceived becomes my Father. Being thus reborn of the Holy Spirit, I have become his son (John 1 :12; 3 : 3–8). Jesus and I are brothers, one in our common parentage. The Spirit of Jesus now animates my own mind. I am in him; he is in me; we are both in the Father (John 14 : 20–23). One of my favorite verses in the New Testament is 1 John 3 : 2: "Beloved, we are God's children already; it does not yet appear what we shall be, but we know that . . . we shall be like him!" This is my hope as a Jesus-person; in fact, it is my only hope. To me, nothing else matters but becoming perfectly obedient to the Creator's will in the same way Jesus was perfectly obedient to that will. The Apostle Paul said, "For me, to live is Christ" (Philippians 1 : 21). I can say the same. Every committed Jesus-man can say the same. Paul also said it another way, "It is no longer I who live, but Christ who lives in me" (Galatians 2 : 20).

In the two previous sections of this book I pointed out that Zen Enlightenment is primarily an experience; all the words written about it simply point to that experience. The same is true of following the Jesus Way. The whole thing is an experience of the Spirit of Jesus, the Holy Spirit, dwelling within the mind of the believer. It is a happening, not a vocabulary. I entered the Jesus Way about thirty years ago. Looking back over those years I can plainly see that I am gradually being changed into his likeness by the presence of his Spirit, the Creator's Spirit, in me. When I first decided to trust my life to him it was like boarding the Japan Air Lines plane in San Francisco. The flight is still in progress. There is turbulence from time to time, but the plane has not faltered. Already I can make out the dim outline of Tokyo Tower in the distance. My initial act of trust is being confirmed in the facts of experience. My faith is being transformed into knowledge. With the Apostle Paul I can say with utter certainty, "I *know* whom I have *believed*" (2 Timothy 1 : 12).

• 28 •

SINCE the final goal of the Jesus Way is the transformation of those who walk it into the likeness of their Lord, the definitive elements of his character must reveal the true nature of perfected man. If those elements were distilled and given verbal formulation, that formulation would constitute what might be called the laws of human nature. Galileo and the scientists who built upon his findings have given verbal and mathematical descriptions of the gravitational forces which govern the relationship between bodies of matter. These descriptions are called the laws of gravity. Some of the most profound mysteries of modern science concern the invisible realities behind these laws. Suppose a man should decide that talk of laws governing such unseen forces is all nonsense made up by some crackpot professors to keep people from having a good time. Forthwith, he steps off the top of a high building resolving to walk on air. It is clear in such a case that any attempt to ignore the laws of gravity cannot succeed. One who tries to break them will inevitably be broken by them. When I say the character of Jesus manifests the laws of human nature, I am speaking of laws just as real, just as absolute, just as unbreakable as the laws of gravity. Any slightest violation of these spiritual laws results necessarily in corresponding damage to the personality of the violator.

This is the import of such unpleasant Biblical statements as "The soul who sins shall die" and "The wages of sin is death" (Ezekiel 18 : 4; Romans 6 : 23). One of my Buddhist friends who is well acquainted with the Christian scriptures called my attention to these two verses and expressed the opinion that such gloomy talk represented the weakness of the Biblical message. Zen releases one from belief in the reality of such things as sin and death.

In the Christian understanding, a man's "soul" is not some sort of gaseous substance which floats out of his body like a ghost when he dies. The soul of a man is his essential spiritual or mental or psychological self: his individual Ego. The death which occurs when a soul sins is not usually physical. Few drop dead from spiritual sins. It is true that the psychosomatic wholeness of an Ego makes physical illness a possible by-product of such sins. But the main damage done by missing the target of being like Jesus is to the mind, the personality, the soul of the sinner.

It follows that what is called divine "punishment" for sin is not some unrelated event like being struck by lightning, but is rather the rending of the delicate fiber of the human psyche. Sins against the body are to refuse it sufficient sleep or wholesome foods, or to stuff it with too much candy or too much milk or whatever. Neglect or carelessness or abuse of the body's mechanisms bring corresponding illnesses, disabilities, and suffering. These maladies are the Creator's "punishment" for such transgressions. In the same way, when a man does an un-Christlike thing such as harboring hatred for someone he believes has wronged him, the psychological damage and mental anguish resulting from his hate is divine "punishment" for his infraction of a law of human nature.

Now it is important to notice that such punishment is instructive. It is not punitive, but rehabilitative. Think what it would be like if infractions against one's real nature were accompanied by no pain. The ache of a broken bone is a cry for cure; the ache of a guilty conscience is a plea for treatment. In each case, the sufferer is made aware that something needs setting right. If the nerves are deadened, one could go walking on unaware of the tearing of the tissues, the splintering of bone, until at last the leg would collapse, beyond repair. So long as one can experience the pain of sin, either against the body or against the soul, there is hope of healing through sought cure. The agonies of war ought to teach mankind something.

BELIEVING as I do that the laws of human nature are revealed in the life of Jesus—believing, in other words, that he lived without sinning against the realities of his personality—I must raise the question, what are the distinctive qualities of his personality of which those laws consist? They can all be subsumed under the heading Love. Paul says:

> Owe no one anything, except to love one another; for he who loves his neighbor has fulfilled the law. The commandments, "You shall not commit adultery, You shall not kill, You shall not steal, You shall not covet," and any other commandment, are summed up in this

> sentence, "You shall love your neighbor as yourself."
> Love does no wrong to a neighbor; therefore love is the fulfilling of the law. (Romans 13 : 8–10 RSV)

All laws and all commandments which are grounded in reality simply describe how Love manifests itself in human conduct.

For Christians, the crucial point is this: Jesus is the perfect embodiment of Love; he himself is the living definition of Love. The English word "love" is so ambiguous it is almost meaningless. When Jesus said, "Love one another as I have Loved you," the meaning became scientifically precise. I am using Love capitalized as the technical term denoting Jesus-Love.

But I must do more than that. To achieve complete clarity regarding this all-important concept, I wish to make use of three Greek words from the New Testament whose meaning is distinctive, but which are each translated into English as "love." Some of my readers will already be familiar with them; others may be meeting them for the first time. I beg the former group's indulgence as I introduce them to the latter. The words are Eros, Philos, and Agape.[1]

EROS: Eros was originally the name of a Greek deity better known today by his Roman name, Cupid. It forms the root of such English words as "erotic," and obviously refers

[1]Although the terms Philos and Agape almost always accord with my definitions of them in New Testament usage, there are a few cases in which their meaning is interchanged. I will use them with strict consistency in the sense here defined.

Other Greek terms might have been used; for example, there is Stergo, signifying family affection, etc. For the sake of simplicity I have chosen to let Philos include all forms of psychical desire just as I am employing Eros to include all forms of physical desire.

to sexual desire. I will use Eros in its broadest sense to include all kinds of bodily hungers: for food, for drink, for air to breathe, for shelter from the cold, for sexual gratification. When I say, "I love ice cream," I mean I like to eat it. If I follow this craving, there will soon be little of the ice cream left. If the love I have for a woman is solely Eros, it would incite me to take her to please myself regardless of whatever harmful consequences there might be for her.

PHILOS: The significance of Philos is suggested in such English derivations as "philo-sophy," love of knowledge; "philo-logy," love of words; "phil-anthropy," love of man; "Phil-adelphia," love of brothers. In short, it denotes intellectual or esthetic attraction to persons or things which one finds pleasing in some way. It is affection for one's own kind. Philos is love of one's native land, for one's parents or one's children, for one's friends. Philos is the sense of comradeship which develops between persons who like to play golf or tennis together, between persons who share an interest in cooking or music. Even simple familiarity can evoke this sort of feeling. I did not have much in common with the janitor of my college, but after a long vacation it would warm my heart to return and see him there busy at his accustomed tasks. He was part of *my* scene! Philos includes team spirit, that esprit de corps which binds men together against mutual adversaries. Invariably Philos requires its object to be pleasing or self-supportive in some way. It can be clearly distinguished from the biological cravings of Eros; its needs are essentially psychical, not physical. And yet in their pure and isolated form, both Philos and Eros are similar in one important respect: both are I-Need forms of love. Each is an attempt to gratify some requirement of the loving self.

AGAPE (pronounced a-ga-pe): In contrast to Eros and Philos, Agape—Jesus-Love—does not depend upon some attractive or likable or compatible or comforting or reassuring aspect of its object. Agape is sometimes described as Love for the unlovely, but this implies a sort of perverse partiality. Agape is absolutely impartial goodwill toward every type of person whether he be attractive or unattractive, friendly or hostile, pleasant or repulsive, protective or threatening. Agape is like Zen Compassion in one respect: it is directed toward every person, just as he is. Agape differs from Compassion in at least three ways: (1) it is directed only toward persons; (2) it requires that the I and the Thou in the Agape-relationship be separate individuals in genuine encounter; and (3) although Agape welcomes each person just as he is, it tries to change him into what he ought to be. Agape does nothing which is not redemptive; that is, everything Agape does is intended to lead those it touches Jesus-ward. But it is never compulsive. It never attempts to overthrow the self-determination of the Thou of its encounter. Agape requires voluntary response.

Above everything else, Agape wills both to perceive and to supply the true needs of the encountered Thou. Often what the other person wants is quite different from what he ought to receive. Agape does not try to please its Thou; Agape seeks only to heal its Thou. It is absolute You-Need Love. The more deeply one enters into the mind of Jesus and senses the motivation behind his words and deeds, the more perfectly one comprehends the meaning of Agape. Jesus *is* Agape!

Yes. Jesus is Agape. The New Testament says, "God is Agape" (*Ho Theos agape estin*—1 John 4 : 16). Since it also says that Jesus is the exact likeness of the Father, it follows that Jesus is what the Father is. "Jesus is Agape!" Every distinctive characteristic of Jesus is an aspect of Agape. The definition of Agape is Jesus himself.

• 30 •

SINCE Jesus himself is the definition of Agape, I wish to call attention to some of his teachings on the subject. In Matthew 5 : 44f. he says:

> Love your enemies and pray for those who persecute you, so that you may be sons of your Father who is in heaven; for he makes his sun rise on the evil and on the good, and sends rain on the just and on the unjust. (RSV)

Here Jesus states that the Agape of the Father-Creator is as free of discrimination as sunlight or rain. The life-giving rays of the sun do not examine a man's moral credentials before they shine on him; drops of rain do not refuse to fall on thirsty fields because the fellow who farms them beats his wife. The Father-Creator *is* Agape; therefore, his gifts are offered with no partiality whatsoever.

In the words just quoted, Jesus is saying, in effect, that men who have been born of the Father's Agape-Spirit will Love one another with the same impartiality as his. Consequently, they can be called his sons only if they are becoming like him in this way. The distinctive mark of all true Jesus-people is, therefore, their readiness to serve their foes as well as their friends. Eros helps those who are likely to reciprocate by satisfying some hunger of the body; Philos helps those it enjoys pleasing; Agape helps those who are in need regardless of the consequences to the one motivated by it.

Agape is You-Need Love. Its activating factor is the discovery of some weakness or deficiency in its object which it has the means to overcome. The attractiveness or unattractiveness of that object is simply of no consequence. Agape is devoid of sentiment. When motivated by Agape, a Jesus-man is just not interested in his own feelings; his attention is focused upon supplying the need of the other person to the exclusion of his own likes and dislikes in the matter. There is a kind of ego-death involved. In the words of Paul, when a Jesus-man has lost himself in Agape he can say, "It is no longer I who live, but it is Christ who lives in me" (Galatians 2 : 20 TEV). This ego-death is a necessary prerequisite to reflecting indiscriminately the sunlight of the Creator's Agape. As long as one's willingness to help another is conditioned by one's own feelings toward that person, the impartiality of Agape is impossible.

*

A second well-known example of Jesus' teaching about Agape is his affirmation of its centrality in perfected man. Here is *the* law of human nature. Only as one becomes such a person does he truly begin to live. Jesus says:

> You shall Love the Lord your God with all your heart, and with all your soul, and with all your mind. This is the great and first commandment.
> And a second is like it, You shall Love your neighbor as yourself.
> On these two commandments depend all the law and the teachings of the prophets. (Matthew 22 : 37–40)

Since God is Love, to Love him means to Love Love. The significance of Jesus' first commandment is, therefore, that one should open himself—heart, soul, and mind—to the indwelling presence of the Creator's Agape-Spirit. There should be no reservations, no holding back. I have said before that my personal hope as a Jesus-man is to be remade by my Creator into the perfect likeness of Jesus. When that process has been completed, then at last all my heart, all my soul, all my mind shall be ruled by Agape. What Jesus gives as the first law of human nature is, in fact, a portrait of his own mind. He already *is* what he here proclaims his followers must finally become!

The second commandment is not essentially different from the first. As Jesus says, it is "like it." To be open to the Creator's Love is to be his instrument in manifesting that Love to men. In the words of John,

> If any one says, "I Love God," and hates his brother, he is a liar; for he who does not Love his brother whom he has seen, cannot Love God whom he has not seen. And this commandment we have from him, that he who Loves God should Love his brother also.
>
> (1 John 4 : 20f.)

In actual practice then, Agape toward the Creator is showing impartial goodwill toward men. In the familiar parable of the Good Samaritan, Jesus describes the Christian's "neighbor" as anyone in need who is within the Christian's reach. To Love this neighbor "as yourself" is to be as sensitive to his sufferings and necessities as to one's own.

An interesting point of contrast with Zen Compassion arises here. A Zen-man accepts his neighbor as himself; that is, as literally identical to himself. Both the self and the neighbor are No-thing-Selves; both are Only-Mind. For Zen, impartial goodwill toward a neighbor is goodwill toward one's self: "I am everything!"

A Jesus-man, on the other hand, feels impartial goodwill toward his neighbors while believing them to be truly other than himself. These neighbors may be antagonistic or loathsome; he might never be able to feel Philos for them. Agape is, however, indifferent to the personal sentiments of the one doing the Loving. As already stated, Agape is activated by awareness of the neighbor's needs, not one's own. A man empowered by Agape has as his sole objective to show the Creator's Agape-Spirit to his neighbor, to release Agape-power into the situation in such a way as to alter it Jesus-ward.

To Love one's neighbor as one's self is also to Love one's self as one's neighbor. Since, by Jesus' explanation, proximity is a necessary characteristic of the "neighbor," one's self becomes a prime object of Agape. Who could be nearer? Showing Agape toward the self requires an impartial and objective evaluation of the self's genuine needs. It demands a scrupulous, unbiased, and realistic meeting of those needs regardless of selfish sentiments. Whether one is showing Agape to one's self or to others, one does the Jesus-like thing. There is no place for self-indulgence when one practices Agape toward one's self.

• 31 •

CONTINUING an examination of Jesus' teaching about Agape, I wish to show how different it is from the sentimental, I-Need emotions which are an integral part of Eros and of Philos. Agape has no desire to keep things sweet and gentle. It is as abrasive as granite, for its substance is absolute truth. It will tolerate no shading, no compromise, no caution of expediency.

Agape engenders a relentless and unbending hate. Yes. Love hates! The perfect incarnation of Agape says:

> If anyone comes to me and does not hate his own father and mother and wife and children and brothers and sisters, yes, and himself as well, he cannot be my disciple. Whoever does not bear his own cross and come after me, cannot be my disciple. (Luke 14 : 26f.)

Elsewhere, speaking on the same subject, he adds:

> Do not think that I have come to bring peace on earth; I have not come to bring peace, but a sword. For I have come to set a man against his father, and a daughter against her mother . . . and a man's foes will be those of his own household. . . . He who finds his life will lose it, and he who loses his life for my sake will find it. (Matthew 10 : 34–39 RSV)

Agape hates! It hates everything which violates Agape! Agape is grounded in Absolute Reality. It is the Spirit of the Creator; hence, it is the essential substance of all his creations. It is Ultimate Truth. It must, therefore, hate every slightest insinuation of what is false or illusory or deceptive or hypocritical. When motivated by Agape, a man will hate any influence brought to bear upon him by members of his family to turn aside from the demands of Agape. When the father or mother of a Jesus-man calls upon him to feel superiority because of ancestral nobility or social position or racial difference, he will hate every aspect of such false posturing. When a parent or a child or a brother or a wife tries to cloak Agape's awareness of the truth in a veil of this kind, the Jesus-man will rip it to shreds. Family pressures toward what is expedient and profitable, rather than toward what is Jesus-like, will be rejected even if a complete rift of family ties is the result. The pages of church history are cluttered with instances of family opposition to those who dedicated themselves to the Jesus Way. The "sword" Jesus came to bring is Agape. It is forever at war with every form of Lovelessness.

In the first passage given above, Jesus properly includes one's own self among those whom one must hate if one would Love. Just as the Agape-man must resist others who would urge him to do the safe, respectable, pleasing thing, rather than the Loving thing, he must also resist every Loveless inclination and selfish appetite he finds within himself. Jesus likens this denial of one's own selfish itches and urges to carrying a cross.

The archetypal act of Agape was Jesus' death upon the cross. The actual death was merely a consequence of his decision to let it happen. That decision itself was the consummating deed of Agape; the physical event was nothing more than its result. Knowing his enemies would try to kill him, knowing also that he could easily escape from them if he chose, Jesus prayed the model prayer of Agape: "Father, if you are willing, remove this cup from me; nevertheless not my will, but yours, be done" (Luke 22 : 42).

Here in Jesus' own life is a perfect example of what it means to Love God with all one's heart and mind and soul. It means giving Agape absolute priority over Eros and Philos. On the level of Eros, Jesus wanted to live. He took no masochistic pleasure in pain. On the level of Philos, Jesus wanted to live. He had congenial friends and a loving mother whose pleasant company he had no wish to leave. He prayed that the "cup" of the crucifixion might be taken from him.

But he gave Agape uncompromising priority over Eros and Philos. The single prayer of Agape is contained in these eight words: "Nevertheless, not my will, but yours, be done!" When any man is ruled by Jesus-Agape, his decisions no longer rest upon his personal feelings. In honesty he will neither hide those feelings, nor hide from them, but he will not let them determine the course of his actions. On the level of Eros and Philos, he wants all manner of things, dreads all manner of things. He hears a jangle of inner voices —their whispers, their screams—but he responds to only one voice: that of Jesus-Agape.

I have a friend on the level of Philos who frequently asks me if I enjoy doing this or that, asks if I enjoy being with this person or that. My reply is: I am most "in joy" when I am least concerned with "enjoyment." This may sound like double-talk, but to me it expresses with almost scientific precision the character of the Agape life. I do not believe Jesus "enjoyed" being murdered on the cross; I believe he was "in joy" as he yielded himself to the will of the Father of Agape to be murdered on the cross. I think this is what Jesus meant in the quotation which opened this chapter: "He who loses his life for my sake will find it." Whenever a man disregards—puts to death—his selfish urge to "enjoy" and, instead, submits his will to Jesus-Agape, he will be most fully alive; he will be "in joy"!

• 32 •

I WANT to reemphasize the Christian belief that living a life motivated by Agape brings one into harmony with ultimate reality. When Agape happens in me, I am submitting myself to the elemental powers of the universe; the Creator is performing his creative acts through me. When my feelings, thoughts, words, and deeds are under the control of the Creator's Agape-Spirit, I am what Paul calls a living "temple of God" (1 Corinthians 3 : 16). At such a time, I can be said to "have the mind of Christ" (1 Corinthians 2 : 16).

But Agape is impossible to achieve by my own efforts. What starts with myself must, one way or another, intend the gratification of myself; the motivation must be I-Need love, must be either Eros, or Philos, or some combination of the two. Agape is possible only when I am in an attitude of dependent receptivity. A respected Christian writer, Emil Brunner, has likened this attitude to an arrow which is held to the string of a tightly drawn bow. The arrow itself is powerless, passive, resting submissively in the archer's grip. Released, it will fly by his might and his aim. When I am that arrow and the Creator that archer, the might and the aim are Agape. This attitude of dependent receptivity is what Christians mean by "faith in God."

What I have just said is clearly implied in the fundamental Biblical presupposition, "God is Agape." By itself, the word "God" is even more ambiguous than "love." "God" can signify as many different supernatural beings as the human mind can imagine. In its Greek form, *theos*, it was applied to a vast number of deities, some of whom were cruel, some of whom were lustful, most of whom were arbitrary in their actions. One of them was Eros. The Japanese term for God, *kami*,[1] designates all manner of nature deities—the

[1]Kami 神; also pronounced *shin*: from the Chinese, *shen*, meaning "good spirits." Kami is used to translate God in the Japanese Bible.

sun, the sea, mountains, rivers, stones, animals, birds—and also includes the spirits of human beings both living and dead. There is a special expression to indicate the vast number of these deities: *yaoyorozu no kami-gami* (myriads of gods).

My point is this: Jesus-people have no stake in a belief in "God" in a general sense. The word becomes useful only if it is understood to have the limited and precise meaning implied in the statement, "God is Agape." This is the only God-concept which is valid for Christians: God is ultimate being; his essential character is Jesus-like. Since all being is derived from his being, the perfected form of everything which exists would express and support Agape. A human being fulfills his reason for being only when he is a submissive instrument of Agape. Only when he is thus born of the Spirit of God can he be called a son of God.

I particularly want to draw attention to the following New Testament passage. Here, in compact form, is found most of what I have been trying to say about the Christian faith so far:

> Love is from (out of) God, and he who Loves is born from (out of) God and knows God.
> He who does not Love does not know God, for God is Love.
> In this was the Love of God made visible among us, that God sent his only Son into the world.
> By this we know that we abide in him and he in us, because he has given us of his own Spirit.
> God is Love, and he who abides in Love abides in God, and God abides in him.
> If any one says, "I Love God," and hates his brother, he is a liar. (1 John 4 : 7–20, selected)

Throughout the original of this passage, the various forms of the word Love are derivatives of the Greek Agape.

What I ask you to notice especially about the quotation is its indication that a man can abide in God and have God abide in him, or not! It states plainly that a person is capable of not Loving, and accordingly, of not knowing God. "He who does not Love does not know God." Furthermore, it says anyone who believes he knows God, but has hatred in his heart, is practicing self-deception. Darkness and light cannot share the same space, for darkness is the absence of light; God and hate cannot share the same mind, for hate is the absence of God. God is Agape, and hate is the absence of Agape.

I have said previously that sin is missing the target of Agape. Every thought, every deed not under God's control is sin. Sensitive Christians find that most of the things they do contain fluctuations of sin. Every time they take the initiative in their actions rather than to rest in the Archer's hands, they sin. There are some people who simplistically equate being a Christian with trying to be kind to others. Quite to the contrary, self-originating efforts to be kind are themselves sinful. What I try to do is I-centered: when I succeed, I am proud; when I fail, I am humiliated. Everything *I* attempt is either from Eros or from Philos. Paul puts it this way: "Even if I give away all I have to feed the poor . . . but have not Agape, it means nothing at all!" (1 Corinthians 13 : 3)

*

Is it not as clear as the sun in the sky that such beliefs are diametrically opposed to the presuppositions of Zen? What does Zen have to do with the notion that ultimate reality is of one specific quality—Agape—and only supports the sort of human-conduct which derives from this? From the standpoint of Enlightenment, what could be more idiotic than to believe—seriously to believe—that there are individual persons who can willfully submit to the indwelling of the Mind of the Universe or not? Ridiculous! There is no division between Only-Mind and the individuals of its universe. Only-Mind is everything. There is no special quality which characterizes Only-Mind; all qualities are its qualities. And all qualities are No-thing.

On Zen presuppositions, my beliefs must be judged nonsense. But to me as a Jesus-man, such beliefs are the foundation upon which my life is established: God is Agape; Jesus is the definition of Agape; faith is submitting to Agape; sin is resisting Agape. Such propositions are not merely arbitrary embellishments which I could discard and yet remain a Christian. They are the *sine qua non* of the Jesus Way.

• 33 •

I HOPE it is now clear why I could not continue to call myself a Christian if I abandoned my conviction that Jesus is uniquely "the way, the truth, and the life." And is it not plain that so long as I hold this conviction, I must agree with Jesus' assertion, "No one comes to the Father, but by me" (John 14 : 6)?

In this connection, I wish to correct a misunderstanding I have encountered in some Buddhist circles, namely, that Christians think they are better than adherents of other faiths. The belief that Jesus is the only perfect revelation of the Father-Creator in no sense gives the believer cause for feeling personal superiority over non-Christians.

It was not through some unusual strength of character on my part that I came to know Jesus. Far from it! For most of the first twenty years of my life I was exclusively motivated by Eros and Philos. I knew nothing of Agape. My life was a restless quest for pleasure. The chief aim of my academic studies was gainful employment after graduation. At the moment I discovered Jesus, there was not one virtue in me to which I could point with pride. The perfection was in him; I brought nothing to the meeting but the eyes to see what he was; these "eyes" themselves were mine only as his gift. The quality of his character was in no way conditioned by the quality of my character. He was what he was; all I did was to discover what he was.

In the same manner, Columbus discovered America. It had been there all the time, with its mountains and plains and rivers and forests. Its breadth and abundance were in no way dependent upon the bodily strength or moral integrity of Columbus. All he did was to find what was already there. It would have existed just as surely if he had never found it. There was no contributory relationship between the character of Columbus and the character of the American continent; its vastness and beauty were in no sense an occasion for Columbus to feel some sort of personal superiority. That vastness and beauty existed with no help from him.

The analogy is, I think, a sound one. If Jesus is—as Christians believe—the only perfect revelation of the Creator, he is this whether they believe it or not. Their belief does not make him so; unbelief does not make him not so. He is what he is. Furthermore, he is what he is regardless of the strengths and weaknesses of those who have come to know him. Whether the person who discovers him is moral or immoral, Jesus is what he is. There is absolutely nothing about finding Jesus which gives the finder reason to feel superior to anyone. The perfection of Jesus exists with no help from the finder.

In my own personal experience I know that meeting Jesus was in no way conditional upon some strength in me. The Continent of Jesus-Agape had been there all the while. I made no contributions to its being. I simply found what had been there all along, what would have been there even had I not found it. As I already said, I was almost twenty when I came upon this World. What a surprise! How unexpected! Ever since, I have been exploring its fascinating "rocks and rills," its "woods and templed hills":[1] exploring the vast Continent of Christ! The more I see, the more enthralled I become! There is nothing here for which I can take credit or feel pride. It is pure and simple discovery on my side; the discovered wonders are all on the side of Jesus-Agape. Everything I do now—whether in or out of Agape—confirms and enriches my understanding of its realities.

I'll say it again: the Christian's belief that Jesus is the unique and perfect revelation of the Father in no sense implies that the Christian himself should feel superior to non-Christians.

*

There is another misunderstanding about the Jesus Way I would like to correct. It fits in well with the analogy of exploring the Continent of Christ, of discovering the wonders of Agape-Reality. I have talked with Buddhists who have

[1]"I love thy rocks and rills / Thy woods and templed hills." From the song "America," by Samuel F. Smith.

the impression that the Jesus Way is one of ascetic renunciation. What I have heretofore said regarding Eros and Philos has doubtless reinforced that impression.

It has been my special delight to observe what happens to Eros and Philos once they fall under the Lordship of Jesus-Agape. Like everything else, apart from him, their uses are perverted; in him, they are fulfilled!

The joys of Eros no longer cloy or debilitate, but satisfy deeply: sex, food, drink; all the sights and sounds of this majestic cosmos, all nature's moods; every color, taste, scent, touch—all the body's hungers and sensations—vibrate in harmony with the omnipresent Agape-Spirit of the Creator. Sexual experience is a hallowed opportunity for self-giving. The taste of food is an occasion for thanksgiving to the Author both of that taste and of my capacity to enjoy it.

Of course, I fall into self-assertive Eros: into lusting instead of Loving; into gluttony instead of gratitude. And every time I fall from Agape, I alight with a thud in a stale, pale phantom-land where I am as a dead man among the dead.

Philos, like Eros, finds its proper function when held steadily in the hand of Agape. I can be a better friend to the people I like, because my liking is conditioned by the sort of objective goodwill which enables me to tell the truth they need to hear, instead of the flattery they would enjoy. By the power of Agape, I can seek a friend's good, rather than his pleasure.

Best of all, Agape enables me to serve those who are offensive to my esthetic sensibilities, those who are hostile toward me, those with whom I strongly disagree. With Philos subservient to Agape, I am empowered not only to be a better friend to my friends, but also—in a miraculous way—to be a genuine friend to my foes. A gratifying result is seeing, again and again, the coldness of hostility thaw into warm friendship as the flame of Agape plays upon them.

When Eros and Philos are on their own, they produce conflict, dissatisfaction, destruction; when Eros and Philos are firmly under the control of Agape, they produce reconciliation, peace, exciting creativity. Christians are certainly against the former; the latter is precisely the Jesus Way. There is nothing ascetic or world-denying about Agape. Everything is affirmed in its created context.

*

This has been a chapter to correct misunderstandings. (1) Jesus-people believe he is the unique revelation of the Father; this does not make them feel superior to anybody. (2) Agape is not asceticism; it is finding where the fun is.

• 34 •

MOST OF the doctrines of Christian theology can be deduced from the presuppositions which I have expanded in the previous chapters of this section. Those presuppositions can be summarized as follows: the character of the Creator-God is Jesus-like Agape; to know Jesus is to know Agape, and this is to know the Creator-God; when created beings are under the control of Agape, they are fulfilling their reason for being; all nonhuman creatures are incapable of self-determination, hence are without moral responsibility; human creatures have the power of self-determination and, therefore, must choose between giving themselves to the domination of Eros and Philos, or to the domination of

Agape; to reject Agape is sin; to choose Agape is righteousness; sin leads to emptiness and death; righteousness leads to joy and peace and life.

*

For the sake of those who may begin to read the New Testament for themselves, I wish to define some of the key terms they will find there. In the light of what has already been said, this can be done briefly.

RIGHTEOUSNESS: What the Creator wills is "right." Since his will is invariably Agape, "right-eousness" is always some aspect of Jesus-like Love. A man's conduct is righteous when it manifests this Love, that is, when he is obeying his Creator's will.

THE RIGHTEOUSNESS OF GOD: This is often used as a technical expression in the letters of Paul. It concerns the means by which God puts men right with himself. All men are sinners; all men have violated the Agape-Spirit. And yet, when one of them decides to entrust himself to the Father of Agape, that one is welcomed just as he is. He is put right with the Father because of his trust. His faith in God's Love is accepted as a substitute for his ability to Love. His willingness to open himself to the re-creating power of God's Love is taken in lieu of his actual capacity to Love. "The righteousness of God" is, therefore, the righteousness which God imputes to a sinner who is still in his sins. Once a Loveless one has been put right with the Lord of Love, both his sense of guilt for his sins and his sense of pride for his virtues are erased. He has become the passive arrow in the Archer's hands. His flight into Love is by the Archer's power, not his own.

RECONCILIATION: Another word for being put right with the Father is reconciliation. At first, a man feels enmity toward God. He feels that his personal independence will be threatened if he draws too near to Omnipotent Love. Whether consciously or not, he tries to flee what he takes to be the Foe of his own selfhood. Like the son in Jesus' parable, he grabs his Father's gifts and goes to a country as far as possible from his Father's presence. He will do as he pleases! He will not be ruled by his Father's will!

Reconciliation occurs when such a man comes to himself, realizes he belongs at his Father's side, and returns to him. Once a man decides to go home, he will see the Father running to meet him. The Father will embrace him joyfully. The son will henceforth live in his proper place; he will be at home.

ATONEMENT: The price Jesus paid to bring men into reconciliation with the Father was his whole life. Daily he allowed his Father to put his selfish impulses to death. Every moment of every day he put I-Need love—Eros and Philos—under the Lordship of You-Need Love. He lived in perfect obedience to Agape. The consummation of such a life was willing submission to his enemies' desire to murder him. This surrender to death upon the cross was not qualitatively different from any other act of Agape. It was merely one more deed of obedience to his Father's will. And yet in its finality, it is the most impressive single thing he did as a slave to Agape. "Greater Agape has no man than this, that he lay down his life" for the objects of his Agape (John 15 : 13). It is the ultimate gift; Jesus gave it.

It was this gift, along with a whole lifetime of giving himself, which constitutes the price he paid to accomplish a reconcilation between human creatures and their Creator. When a man begins to understand who Jesus was and what he did, that man gets his first glimpse of pure Agape. Measured by its standard, he realizes two things simultaneously:

(1) what he ought to be, and (2) what he is. He *ought* to be like Jesus; he *is* a sinner. This vision of reality starts him on his journey home to the Father. The Father has been yearning for his return, but could not coerce him without violating the very heart of Agape. Any deed of Agape is one of free self-determination. Jesus died to selfishness daily—finally, on the cross—to pay the price necessary to reconcile men to God. In the words of Paul:

> God shows his Agape for us in that while we were yet sinners, Christ died for us. . . . While we were enemies, we were reconciled to God by the death of his Son. (Romans 5 : 8, 10)

Peter stated the same belief:

> He himself bore our sins in his body on the cross, that we might die to sin and live to righteousness. By his wounds you have been healed. For you were straying like sheep, but have now returned to the Guardian of your true selfhood. (1 Peter 2 : 24f.)

Human creatures like you and me murdered Perfect-Agape. Those who came to realize what they had done were aghast at the awfulness of their deed, were broken to repentance, were brought to the Father of Agape yearning to be healed of their hate and re-created into his image. And it is precisely this attitude of yearning which opens the human heart to the inpouring of the power of Agape. In Biblical terms, such a one is filled with the power of the Holy Spirit. That power does the rest. The remaking of the personality into the likeness of Jesus is the Holy Spirit's job.

FORGIVENESS OF SINS: Forgiveness is the willingness of

Perfect Love to overlook truly repented acts of Lovelessness. Jesus says a condition for being forgiven is the willingness to forgive. Refusal to forgive is refusal to Love; refusal to Love is the essence of impenitence; Love is constitutionally incapable of forgiving unrepented Lovelessness. The psychological effect of divine forgiveness is to relieve the sinner from the burden of his past and allow him to move forward unhindered into Christlikeness under the transforming power of Creator-Agape.

REPENTANCE FOR SINS: The literal meaning of repentance is to change one's mind. It includes both revulsion at one's acts of self-centeredness and a profound craving to be lifted out of them. It is the attitude which opens the ego to the unmaking and remaking might of Agape's Holy Spirit.

HOLINESS; SAINT; SANCTIFICATION: The Greek root for these three terms is *hagios*, meaning to set something aside for special use. My father had a large leather chair. When he came home, I cleared out of it. All the family regarded that chair as being set aside for his exclusive use whenever he wanted it. In the original meaning of the word, it is correct to say that chair was "holy" to my father.

When an individual gives himself over to the exclusive use of Agape, he is holy to Jesus; he is a saint; he is sanctified. In the New Testament, a saint is not some outstanding hero of the faith; from the moment any person has been reconciled to the Father, that person is a saint.

GRACE: From the Greek *charis*—literally, "a gift"—grace is the New Testament word signifying the impartiality of Agape. The Father's gifts of reconciliation, forgiveness, and re-creation of personality are offered indiscriminately to anyone who is willing to receive them. An apparently moral man has no advantage over an obvious sinner. God treats all men alike. When men come under the domination of Agape, they become instruments of this grace; they offer their gifts with the same impartiality to friend and foe alike. Agape always begins on the Godward side. If any man Loves God, "We Love him because he first Loved us" (1 John 4 : 19). This initiating aspect of Agape is grace. Through Love for his enemies, a Jesus-man provokes them into Love responses. This is the methodology of atonement.

THE WRATH OF GOD: As I said in another chapter, Love hates. Agape cannot tolerate even the smallest deviation from Agape into selfishness. Any such deviation is sin. Anything which has about it the slightest scent of self-seeking, anything which smacks of indifference to one's neighbor's needs, anything which has the lightest taint of Eros-domination or Philos-domination, anything which contains the tiniest grain of sham or hypocrisy—any such thing cannot be endured by Agape. And what Agape hates always kindles its wrath.

Jesus demonstrated the wrath of Love when he found merchants in the Temple of Jerusalem busily engaged in gouging high profits from the poor who had come there to worship. Here was Lovelessness being practiced in the very sanctuary which had been set aside for the exclusive use of the Father of Love! See how Perfect Agape responded:

> Jesus went into the Temple and drove out all those who bought and sold in the Temple; he overturned the tables of the money-changers and the stools of those who sold pigeons, and said to them:
> "It is written in the Scriptures that God said, 'My house will be called a house of prayer,' but you are making it a hideout for thieves!" (Matthew 21 : 12f. TEV)

Thus must Love always deal with Lovelessness. But notice

that this act of wrath was, at the same time, an act of Love intended to call the sinful merchants to repentance. Wrath is a face of Love. Just as a doctor hates sickness because he wants his patients healthy, so Jesus hates sin because he Loves sinners and wants to save them from their sin.

In order to emphasize this important point, I will quote some more of Jesus' Love-talk:

> Woe to you, scribes and Pharisees, hypocrites! for you are like whitewashed tombs, which outwardly appear beautiful, but within they are full of dead men's bones and all uncleanness. So you also outwardly appear righteous to men, but within you are full of hypocrisy and iniquity! . . . You serpents, you brood of vipers, how are you to escape being sentenced to hell?
>
> (Matthew 23 : 27f., 33 RSV)

This is a good example of the difference in communication style between Philos and Agape. Under all circumstances, Philos wants to keep things polite and pleasant when dealing with its friends. When its wrath is directed toward its enemies, the purpose is to hurt them. When an important moral issue is at stake, the wrath of Agape will be expressed toward enemies or friends alike—never with the intention of harming, always with the intention of helping. In most circumstances Agape will be genial and courteous, but when blatant Lovelessness is involved, Agape will apply the surgical knife of speaking the hard truth. The tough shell of the hypocrisy-hardened Pharisees would have been impervious to mild reprimand. Jesus dealt with them according to their need.

More often Agape's wrath is tender. This is shown in the following more typical instance of Jesus' manner with sinners. When a woman was caught in the act of adultery and about to be stoned to death by a mob, Jesus shamed the people in the crowd into leaving her alone. When they had all gone away he said to her:

> "Woman, where are they? Has no one condemned you?" She said, "No one, Lord." And Jesus said, "Neither do I condemn you; go, and do not sin again."
> (John 8 : 10f. RSV)

Each of the above examples in its own way reveals an aspect of the wrath of God. It is always a call to repentance. If the call is heeded, the sinner is saved; if the call is disregarded, the sinner has chosen his own condemnation.

THE JUSTICE OF GOD: The justice of Agape is the condemnation of Lovelessness and the commendation of Lovingness. Some have thought that God's justice and his Love are somehow at variance with one another. On the contrary, the diamond hardness of the many-faceted jewel of Agape cuts through all which is not of Agape as surely as a hot knife cuts through butter. Since Jesus is Perfect-Love, his words, his life, his personality are the judgment which sloughs away all which is not Love, and leaves behind a shimmering globe of everlasting reality composed of every thought and every deed which has been Agape-born in the heart of man. I believe those who have difficulty reconciling God's Love and his justice have not yet come to understand the nature of Agape; I believe they have confused Philos with Agape.

If a man persists to the end in locking Love from his life, Love will not overrule his choice. He shall have the eternal absence of Love which he has elected. Since God is Love, and God is the ground of being, the renunciation of Love is the renunciation of God and, therefore, is the renunciation of being. The justice of Love requires this. The essence of Love is freedom of will. It is the nature of Agape neither to tolerate Lovelessness nor to coerce Love; it is the nature of Agape to create Christlikeness in all who choose Love. This is the justice of God.

PRAYER: Jesus-like prayer is not an attempt to change God's mind and cause him to give me what I want; it is, rather, offering my mind to be changed by him to cause me to give him what he wants. Prayer is a deliberate act of my own will to allow the power of Agape to overwhelm the Eros and the Philos in me, thus making them subservient to the Father of Agape.

I have previously given Jesus' model prayer: "If it be possible, let this cup pass from me; nevertheless, not my will, but thine be done." Eros said, Avoid suffering! Philos said, Remain with your friends! Agape said, Bodily pain is not a deciding factor; you can best serve both your friends and your foes by submitting to death. Eros and Philos said, Save yourself! Agape said, Save the world! As a result of prayer, Jesus was enabled both to hear and to heed the voice of Agape.

• 35 •

THE CHASM which exists between such New Testament concepts as Righteousness, Judgment, Holiness, the Wrath of God, the Grace of God, Repentance, Forgiveness, Reconciliation, Atonement, and Prayer, on the one hand, and the Zen presupposition, I am everything and everything is Nothing, on the other, is so vast I hardly need call attention to it. Every one of these New Testament teachings presupposes real individual selves living in a three-dimensional world of tangible matter. They all presuppose otherness between the Creator and all creatures, otherness which is vastly extended in the case of human creatures with their capacity either to obey or to disobey the Creator's Agape-Will. Zen Enlightenment is a deliverance from precisely these assumptions. The tranquility of the Zen Way rests upon the certainty that there is no self and no other, no good to be pursued and no evil to be eschewed.

In particular, Zen sutras and the teachings of Zen masters emphasize the illusory nature of the dread distinction between life and death. I have already quoted the *Hannya-Shin-gyō* on this point:

不 生 不 滅
No coming into being; no ceasing to be.

Another quotation from the same is:

無 生 無 老 死
No-thing birth; No-thing old-age death

"There is no coming into being; there is no ceasing to be." And again, "Birth is No-thing; old age and death are No-thing."

What more effective way to abolish the fear of death than to hold the certainty that one was not born and therefore cannot grow old and die? And this is a thoroughly logical deduction from the Zen presupposition: I am Only-Mind; Only-Mind is everything; everything is No-thing. The new-born baby and the corpse in the coffin are equally dream images of Only-Mind; therefore, they are not three-dimensional things in three-dimensional space. Nothing is outside Only-Mind. Only-Mind itself was not born and does not die.

Only-Mind is forever in the timeless moment of the eternal Now (Ichi-nen).

*

In sharp contrast to the Zen Way of no birth and no death, the Jesus Way takes both individual life and individual death with utter seriousness. Jesus offers deliverance from fear of death not by denying its objective existence, but by his own victory over death through Resurrection. When the New Testament speaks of Last Things—those realities which lie beyond the framework of bodily life in the present, material world—its language is of necessity metaphorical. It is dealing with modes of being beyond the experience of those of us who still live in the flesh. For a man of flesh to require a completely understandable explanation of these things would be something like a five-year-old child demanding a lucid explanation of Einstein's Theory of Relativity. The problem is not with the substantiality of the realities involved, but with the knowing-mechanisms of matter-based mortals.

Do not ask me, therefore, to give a detailed description of a Resurrection Body or of Heaven or of Hell. All I can tell the reader is what the New Testament tells me. And the main thing it says about death is that on the Sunday morning following Jesus' crucifixion, some of his friends came to show respect at his tomb, but found it empty. Later, various ones at different times and under different circumstances said they saw him, talked with him, heard him preach, touched the nail holes in his hands and feet. At the time of Jesus' death, they were in hiding for fear they would meet the same fate. Following the encounter with the resurrected Jesus, they were suddenly changed into brave preachers of the Jesus Way, willing to be beaten, put in prison, and to die rather than to deny him. What brought about this incredible transformation from fear to boldness? Something tremendous must have happened!

Those people themselves said that what made the difference was meeting the risen Jesus.

*

The New Testament further teaches that all people who have yielded themselves to the Agape-Spirit of the Creator will also be raised from death in a resurrection like that of Jesus. Paul says Jesus was the first, but only the first, of an endless procession of human creatures whom the Creator would raise from the tomb. "In Christ shall all be made alive. But each in his own order: Christ the first, then at his Second Coming those who belong to Christ" (1 Corinthians 15 : 22f.).

Although Jesus himself assured his disciples there is no way to know when it will happen, he said he will come a second time to the earth. That Second Coming will be an end to history as men know it now. At that time there will be established "a new earth" (Revelation 21 : 1). It is at the time of this Second Coming that all those who during earthly life have yielded themselves to the Creator's Agape-Power will be resurrected to a new kind of life adapted to the "new earth" which shall then come into being. What kind of body will believers have at that time? Paul says trying to guess this is like trying to predict what sort of plant will grow simply by looking at a seed. As the appearance of the seed is quite different from the gracefully waving stalk of wheat which grows from it, so will the Resurrection Body be quite different from men's mortal bodies. Of the difference between our mortal body and the Resurrection Body he says, "What is sown is perishable, what is raised is imperishable. . . . It is sown in weakness, it is raised in power. It is sown a physical body, it is raised a spiritual body" (1 Corinthians 15 : 42–44 RSV). Now I do not have the faintest idea what a "spiritual body" which is "strong" and "imperishable" will be like. And I go further: I believe anyone who says he does know what that body will be like is fooling himself. Paul's whole point is that the "spiritual body" is beyond imagination. If I had only seen an acorn, but never seen a tree, is there any way I could guess the appearance of an oak?

There is no profit in spending more words on the indescribable. But the graspable realities regarding this resurrection life are stated quite plainly in the New Testament.

There will be an individual "spiritual body" for each person who has experienced reconciliation with the Love-Spirit of his Creator. There will be some sort of "new earth" in which he will dwell. And there will be a quality of life in which each resurrected individual will be exactly like Jesus in character; hence, each will fulfill all the potentialities of his own distinctive personality. This means each will be living in total obedience to the Creator's Agape-Will. One of the most suggestive New Testament descriptions of the general life-style in that "new earth" is this:

> Behold, the dwelling of God is with men. He will dwell with them, and they shall be his people, and God himself will be with them; he will wipe away every tear from their eyes, and death shall be no more, neither shall there be mourning nor crying nor pain any more, for the former things have passed away.
>
> (Revelation 21 : 3f. RSV)

One thing is clear. Heaven is not "Pie in the sky, by and

by." Heaven is not a place up in the heavens, but is a state of being in which individual human creatures will live in perfect harmony both with their Creator and with one another. As Jesus joyfully gave all his abilities to the practice of Agape, so each man who trusts in him will ultimately do the same. In Jesus' most familiar prayer, he prayed, "Our Father. . . . May your will be done on earth, as it is in heaven" (Matthew 6 : 9f.). Heaven is where the Father's will is done. The Kingdom of Heaven is the realm in which the Father of Agape is King.

It follows that if a man has already submitted his will to this King, that man is in the Kingdom of Heaven right here on this present earth. What awaits him beyond death in the Resurrection is just a fulfillment and completion of the Heaven in which he now dwells.

*

Hell is the opposite of Heaven. If Heaven is a state of being in which the Agape-Spirit is obeyed, Hell is a state of being where it is not obeyed. There is a figurative description of a Final Judgment at the time of Jesus' Second Coming in which all people who have ever lived are shown standing before Jesus. It pictures him as separating them into two groups: those who were instruments of Agape, and those who rebelled against Agape. To the latter group he says with great pity and sadness:

> "Depart from me, you cursed, into the eternal fire prepared for the devil and his angels; for I was hungry and you gave me no food, I was thirsty and you gave me no drink, I was a stranger and you did not welcome me, naked and you did not clothe me, sick and in prison and you did not visit me." Then they also will answer,

> "Lord, when did we see thee hungry or thirsty or a stranger or naked or sick or in prison, and did not minister to thee?" Then he will answer them, "Truly, I say to you, as you did it not to even the humblest of men, you did it not to me." And they will go away into eternal punishment. (Matthew 25 : 41–46 RSV, altered)

Those who are sent away from the presence of Jesus are the people who rejected Love. What clearer picture of Lovelessness could be given than this list of refusals to meet their Neighbor's need?

As physical descriptions of Heaven are intended to do no more than suggest modes of being which are far beyond our comprehension so also are those of Hell. Since one of the most intense forms of bodily suffering is that of being severely burned, a searing flame becomes an effective image of that suffering which is experienced when the essential selfhood of a person is warped and distorted out of its intended form through Lovelessness. Man was made to Love as Jesus Loved; as he slips deeper and deeper into anti-Love his own distinctive identity is more and more blurred and deformed. If the final goal of the Jesus Way is to be re-created into his likeness, the final goal of those who renounce that way is total unlikeness to him. This is the Final Punishment described in the previous quotation. Final Punishment is the complete obliteration of the marks of Agape from the personality. It is to hate the Agape-Creator with all one's heart and mind and soul, and to hate one's neighbor as one hates oneself. This is Hell. Paul lists some of the characteristics of the citizens of Hell:

> immorality, impurity, licentiousness, idolatry, sorcery, enmity, strife, jealousy, anger, selfishness, dissension,

> partisan spirit, envy, drunkenness, carousing, and the like. (Galatians 5 : 19–21)

Just as Heaven starts in this present world when a man takes hands off his life and lets Love have control, so also Hell begins here and now with every Loveless choice a person makes. Those characteristics of Hell's citizens mentioned by Paul are acquirable long before death and resurrection. Hell, in the final sense, is simply a ripening of the fruit of the tree of anti-Agape.

It comes down to this. Man gets what he chooses. In likeness to his Creator man was given self-determination. And this is just what he does; he determines the ultimate quality of his own ego. He can choose Agape, and become what he was created to be, like Jesus; he can choose to reject Agape, and be unmade.

> Do not be deceived; Agape-God is not mocked, for whatever a man sows, that he will also reap. For he who sows selfishness will reap the corruption of the self; but he who sows to the Agape-Spirit will from the Agape-Spirit reap eternal life. (Galatians 6 : 7f.)

*

Nowhere is the cleavage between the Zen Way and the Jesus Way more apparent than in the respective attitude of each toward death. To Awaken to Zen Understanding is to know that individual bodies are No-thing; they are not born; they do not die. To choose Jesus-Agape is to expect continuing development into his likeness throughout one's life in a mortal, physical body, and to anticipate the final perfecting of that likeness in an immortal Resurrection Body. The farther a man walks the Zen Way, the more completely all individuality is erased; the farther a man walks the Jesus Way, the more his individuality is sharpened.

• 36 •

WHILE the doctrines of the Jesus Way of Agape presuppose belief in a material world of three-dimensional space and three-dimensional objects, Zen denies the existence of such a world. How could two such mutually exclusive faiths come into being? Both have been held with firm conviction by a large number of adherents, many of whom are not only quite sincere but also of high intelligence.

Most people uncritically accept the reality of an external world as a matter beyond debate. This is the prevalent view of things. Even Zenists started out thinking this way. Only after the experience of Enlightenment do they begin to deny the distinction between the knower and the known. Very few Buddhists ever go so far as to seek Enlightenment. Of those who make the attempt, few succeed. Obviously the men who achieve Enlightenment must be gifted with great tenacity and considerable mental ability. How could persons of such character bring themselves to believe what seems to practical-minded people sheer nonsense?

Is not the quality of men who have achieved Enlightenment clear evidence that the experience they describe must be grounded in some sort of psychological reality? I believe it is. Having met some of these men I cannot doubt their mental capacities and, furthermore, I cannot doubt that they did have an experience which to them was completely convincing. In order to understand them, I sought that experience for myself. I think I have been successful. I have had sustained periods of seeing everything as No-thing. I have experiential understanding of what I believe to be the psychological realities behind the expression, I am Only-Mind and Only-Mind is everything. I have tasted the tranquility of Not-Two and Not-One. I have touched the scent of a flower. I have heard the clap of one hand.

What Zen says about the inadequacy of words to describe the experience is quite true. They are but a finger pointing to the moon. And one will never behold the moon if he becomes fascinated with the finger, instead of turning to what it indicates.

All the Zen terms introduced in Sections I and II direct the attention toward a state of mind which is unquestionably possible to attain. While in that mind state, the world which one perceives is exactly the one the Zen masters describe. From personal encounter with the inner substance of this distinctive mental outlook, I can easily understand the appropriateness of the sort of responses which were given to seekers by the masters of bygone ages and preserved in the Kōan anecdotes. Years ago when I first began to read Zen literature, the antics and exclamations of those masters seemed outrageously irrational. Now I can appreciate the creative genius which enabled them to say the same thing over and over again with such spontaneity, freshness, and pregnant novelty.

*

To set forth the psychological realities upon which I believe Zen Enlightenment stands, I will explain two or three elementary principles of epistemology. For any reader not familiar with the term, epistemology is the science of how the mind knows things. It has long been understood by investigators in this field that any conscious perception is subject to two equally plausible and equally unprovable interpretations: (1) the things perceived are totally a product of the mind which perceives them; (2) the things perceived are a product of the perceiving mind in response to sensory contact with entities external to the mind.

Both interpretations acknowledge that a mind can be conscious only of its own contents. A mind can have immediate knowledge of the images in its own consciousness, nothing more. Zen understands this and dares to believe there *is* nothing more. There is Only-Mind. Zen chooses to trust in the first of the two interpretations.

Most people, on the other hand, are what I will call epistemological Materialists. They believe there is a material world external to their own minds. Most of them fell into this view of things without realizing they were making a choice on pure faith. They were not aware of the epistemological principle stated in the previous paragraph: that a mind can only have immediate knowledge of the contents of its own consciousness. Without ever deliberately doing so, most people have adopted the second interpretation. They take the existence of the external world to be self-evident. Some of my readers may be in this group. At this very moment you may be skeptical of the primary epistemological principle I have just stated. I have said it is impossible for you to see or hear or taste or smell or touch anything directly. All you can have is a subjective experience of these sensations.

You don't believe me? Just think about it a minute. (I'm on your side, remember? I believe the material world is out there just as strongly as you do. But what I want you to realize is that this is a *belief*. It cannot be proved!) Suppose, for example, you see a red ball. You, the seer, are a nondimensional seeing-point inside your brain. What you see—the solidity, the roundness, the redness of the ball—is an image in your consciousness there with you inside your mind.

As a Christian Materialist, I choose to believe that the picture of the ball which you perceive there inside your head is produced as a response of your nervous system to something outside your head. I believe a stream of electronic particles originating from the sun have come through space to strike the surface of a three-dimensional ball (itself a globe of minute molecules in frantic motion). Some of the sun's electronic particles bounce off the ball and ricochet through the hole in your eye, its pupil. Pouring through that hole, and focused by your eye lens, those particles pound upon the sensitive screen of the retina at the back of your eye. This pounding generates a series of electrical impulses which travel along wirelike optical nerve cords to a place where those cords are attached to your brain. Once these pulses of electricity enter your brain, they are transformed by it into a picture which you, the seeing-point inside your brain, perceive as a red ball.

The all-important point I wish to illustrate is quite obvious, once you've seen it. The nearest you, the seeing-point, can get to that red ball is the place where your optic nerve cords attach to your brain. There is no way you can squeeze yourself into those cords, worm your way along them until you enter your eye, look out of its pupil and see things for yourself. There is no way you, there inside your head, can cut a hole through the side of your skull and get a direct look at the world outside. All you or anyone else can ever see is the picture created by the brain in response to electrical impulses reaching it through its nerve-wires. You cannot see your brain. You can never see those nerve-wires themselves. You can never see your eyes. If you cannot even see your own brain, or the wires which run from it to your world-window eyes, if you can never see your own eyes, how can you possibly get a direct look at whatever might be in a world somewhere beyond them? Sorry, it simply cannot be done.

The old expression "Seeing is believing!" is not true in the way it was intended, but it is absolutely true in reverse. If a person thinks "seeing" brings him into contact with objective reality, it is altogether an act of "believing." If you are seeing something outside your own head, it is because you choose to believe it is there. The only evidence you have for the existence of anything whatever is your own subjective mental experience. You can never get outside your mind.

If I may be excused for returning to an improbable illustration given in earlier sections, let me again ask you to pretend you were born and have always lived inside a doorless, windowless room with walls, ceiling, and floor so thick no sound can penetrate them. You are strapped into a chair in such a way that you cannot move your body, your head, or even your eyes. Straight in front of you is a large color TV set with facilities not only for showing pictures with three-dimensional effect, but also stereophonic sound, a device for emitting appropriate scents, a gadget attached to your tongue which produces tastes, and electrodes like those of Huxley's feelies pressed into the palms of your motionless hands, giving you the sensation of touching what you see on the screen.

What a fix you're in! As the days and weeks and years go by, your TV shows you a whole world of people, events. places, and things. Many of these are seen so often you become quite familiar with them. And yet, there is positively no means for you to discover if any of the things your TV set shows you actually exist in a world beyond the walls which surround you. There are two possibilities: (1) the sights, sounds, and other sensations are produced by mechanisms within the set itself as it is activated by some sort of preprogrammed tape; (2) the sights, sounds, and other sensations are reproductions in your TV set of real things in a three-dimensional world outside your small prison cell which are being picked up by cameras, microphones, and other electronic equipment out there with them. Since your knowledge is completely limited to what is showing on the TV, all you can do is to choose between the first and the second possibility by faith. If you select the second, and believe there are actual things outside your tiny chamber which correspond to the pictures you see, there is no way you can ever verify this belief. Even if your faith is correct, you can never get any nearer to that outside world than your TV screen. Seeing is believing; seeing things is an act of believing they are there.

Did I say this illustration was farfetched? I was wrong. You were born inside the doorless, windowless room of your brain. No light, no sound, nothing filters through its walls. The highly advanced TV set, with scent and taste and touch devices added, is your consciousness. You—strapped, immovable, staring straight ahead at the screen—are the seeing-point which is the "I" in such statements as "I see" and "I hear." All you can know directly is the world which appears inside your head.

Although my presentation has been informal, I have been stating scientific fact. My illustration is merely an updating of one given by scientist Karl Pearson in a book called *The Grammar of Science*, published in London back in 1900. He described a switchboard operator in a telephone exchange:

How close then can we actually get to this supposed

world outside ourselves? Just as near but no nearer than the brain terminals of the sensory nerves. We are like the clerk in the central telephone exchange who cannot get nearer to his customers than his end of the telephone wires. We are indeed worse off than the clerk, for to carry out the analogy properly we must suppose him *never to have been outside the telephone exchange, never to have seen a customer or any one like a customer—in short, never, except through the telephone wire, to have come in contact with the outside universe.*

Of that "real" universe outside himself he would be able to form no direct impression; the real universe for him would be the aggregate of his constructs from the messages which were caused by the telephone wires in his office. About those messages and the ideas raised in his mind by them he might reason and draw his inferences; and his conclusions would be correct—for what? For the world of telephonic messages, for the type of messages that go through the telephone. . . . Pent up in his office he could never have seen or touched even a telephonic subscriber *in himself.*

Very much in the position of such a telephone clerk is the conscious *ego* of each one of us seated at the brain terminals of the sensory nerves. Not a step nearer than those terminals can the *ego* get to the "outer world" and what in and for themselves are the subscribers to its nerve exchange it has no means of ascertaining . . .

Reality of the external world lies for science and for us in combinations of form and color and touch—sense-impressions as widely divergent from the thing "at the other end of the nerve" as the sound of the telephone from the subscriber at the other end of the

> wire. We are cribbed and confined in this world of sense-impressions like the exchange clerk in his world of sounds and not a step beyond can we get.[1]

The epistemological principle that you the reader can have direct knowledge of your own consciousness there inside your skull and nothing more is then old stuff to scientists. This precept goes back to Immanuel Kant (1724–1804) and his distinction between Phenomena and Noumena which I explained on pages 31–32. In fact it goes back over two thousand years to the Greek philosopher Plato who taught that the ego is like a man in a cave tied in such a way that he can never turn his head toward the mouth of the cave to see whatever may be outside in the sunshine. All he can see are shadows moving on the inner wall of the cave before his fixed gaze. He supposes those shadows are caused by beings passing to and fro before the entrance, but he can only guess what they are in reality. He can never see anything but the shadows.

If this is new to you it may at first appear to be manifest moonshine. After you have thought it over, you will under-

[1]Quoted by George Stuart Fullerton, *An Introduction to Philosophy* (New York: Macmillan Company, 1908), pp. 38–41. Fullerton was Professor of Philosophy at Columbia University, New York. He is quoting from Karl Pearson, *The Grammar of Science* (London: [Publisher not given], 1900), pp. 60–63. As you see, three full pages are given to the quotation from Pearson. (The italicized words are in the original.) I have given only a short portion of the whole.

I first heard of the illustration in a passing reference by Elton Trueblood in his *Logic of Belief* (New York: Harper and Brothers, 1942), p. 204. It was after that I tracked down the whole in Fullerton. Here is Trueblood's reference:

> My perception of the bird in the tree is as much in my mind as is my perception of God. Strictly speaking every man is like Karl

stand that it is simple fact. The only thing you can know directly is what goes on inside your brain. Everything else is guesswork.

*

There is, then, a solid psychological basis for the Zen premise, "I am Only-Mind; Only-Mind is everything; everything is No-thing."

As an epistemological Materialist, I believe in the existence of an external world. But I cannot prove it. My Zen friends believe that mind-images are wholly mind-made. But they cannot prove it. Each of us has the same raw data: the contents of his own consciousness. With all my heart, I am committed to the conviction that there is a three-dimensional universe filled with animate and inanimate beings. With all their hearts, my Buddhist friends are committed to the conviction that there is nothing outside the Mind. So far as the verifiable evidence goes, there is just as much to support their view as there is to support mine. Neither their belief nor mine can be proved; neither can be disproved.

> Pearson's imagined telephone operator, locked forever in his windowless exchange, but supplied with wires connecting him with what he takes to be an outside world. He cannot know for sure that there is an outside world. Even if he checks his messages by reference to the experience of another operator in another room, he has not escaped his "egocentric predicament" because this added evidence comes in what is merely another wire. Why should he trust his ideas about what purports to be a second operator any more than his ideas about the twentieth subscriber?

For the sake of emphasizing the central point of my present chapter, let me call your attention to the sentence, "He cannot know for sure that there is an outside world."

Both the Materialistic Pluralism which is a basic premise of the Jesus Way and the Idealistic Non-Dualism which is a fundamental presupposition of Zen are based entirely on faith.

Man can only have immediate knowledge of the contents of his own mind. This is the epistemological reality which lies behind Zen's belief in Only-Mind.

• 37 •

SINCE I can only have immediate knowledge of what happens inside my mind and have no way to ascertain that there is a world outside it, all I need in order to experience Zen Satori is to realize this existentially. It is one thing to understand the mental quality of objects intellectually, but quite another to understand it experientially. I said earlier I have learned how to induce the psychological experience which I believe is the essence of Enlightenment. If the reader would like to try an experiment I have found useful to this end, here it is:

Stand in a room facing a large plate-glass window. Pretend that the window is a mirror. Imagine that everything you can see through it—the lawn, the trees, the birds, the cars passing in the street, the neighbor mowing the grass across the road, your children playing in your front yard—pretend that all these outdoor things are not actually outdoors, but are images in the glass of your window, the mirror. Pretend further that these things are not reflections of objects external to the mirror, but are mysteriously generated within the mirror itself.

Next, go closer until you can touch the glass surface and

feel its perfect motionlessness. Despite the swaying of the windblown trees, the swift flight of birds, and all the movement you behold in the mirror's depth, nothing moves!

One thing more. Stand so close to the glass that you can no longer see the borders of the window. As it were, move into the mirror, or rather take the mirror into your mind. Now all you can perceive is the mirror. But you do not see the mirror itself; what you see is the pattern of "reflections" which the mirror is creating before the eye of your awareness.

If you are successful in these pretenses you will actually begin to *feel* that the things before you are nonobjective, are mirror-born, are mind-born. What you are viewing is the mirror, nothing but the mirror. What you see specifically is the images within it, but those images are, in fact, the mirror itself. Can you put your hand into a mirror and seize upon any of the things you see there? Clearly, a mirror and its images are Not-Two. If your pretense with the window has been successful, you will *feel* that the things you are seeing are visions inside your mind, as they in fact are. Now this is no longer merely an epistemological principle understood by your intellect; it has become experienced reality.

If you will shut off the analytical processes of your thought—leave aside the whole question of the *cause* of those visions in your mind—and just look upon the things you see as mental images, you will get a direct glimpse into the world of Zen Enlightenment.

It may take some practice to get the full effect, but some years ago I found that this technique will bring on for me a psychological experience of the nonobjectivity or No-thingness of whatever I may be perceiving.

I prefer a window to an actual mirror because a mirror reflects the seer, reflects my own face with its peering eyes.

The ego-spectator in my mind is an unseen seeing-point; I see, but am not seen. It is the same seeing-point (I) who views my sleeping dreams. The I who sees is not my eye. In sleep my eye is closed, but still I see. When I let a window be a mirror, the proper situation is reproduced: while viewing its images, I (the seeing-point) remain invisible.

One can use the glass in his glasses the same way as a window. Conceived as mirrors, the lenses create the same effect as the stationary window in one's living room, with the additional advantage that one can walk along a busy city sidewalk, turn his head this way and the other, can view everything including his own motions as if the whole scene is happening in a mirror. If the experience is right, he will feel that he himself (the seeing-point) is motionless. The sidewalk and the things he passes along the way will flow toward him and fall away behind.

For myself, I no longer need even the glass in my spectacles to conjure up the sensation that I am looking into a mirror. The lenses of my eyes themselves do very well.

*

Some may ask if the Enlightenment experience can be achieved without Za-zen, without emptying the mind through long hours of rigorous concentration upon some Kōan. The Zen masters themselves would answer "Yes." If one can arrive at a genuine experience of the No-thingness of things without the Mind-emptying labors of Za-zen, the Za-zen is not necessary. After all, Only-Mind is never other than the Buddha-Mind. It is for this reason Suzuki said, in the interview quoted in Section II, that the Myōkōnin (Mysterious-Joy-People)[1] of the True Pure Land Sect

[1]Mysterious-Joy-People: J., Myōkōnin 妙好人; literal translation.

are experiencing true Satori. The adherents of that sect do not usually practice Za-zen. They make no effort to empty their minds. They come to their Awakening while engaged in the activities of everyday life. When they begin to sense the presence of Amida in everything, and respond with Thankfulness (Kansha)[2] to whatever happens, the essential realities of the Enlightenment experience are theirs. No need for them to empty their minds.

*

It is quite true, however, that many do get their first glimpse of the world of Enlightenment through emptying the mind by means of Za-zen. Although the easiest way I have found to induce the experience in myself is the mirror pretense just described I have also done a considerable amount of Za-zen. My legs are too long and unbending to let me do the full-lotus position comfortably, but I can sit about an hour in the half-lotus, if my pillow is high enough. (The full-lotus requires that each foot be drawn up through the crook of the opposite leg; the half-lotus, only one foot.)

I can give firsthand testimony to the fact that, with practice, one can reduce the contents of his consciousness down to a single point (it is not a point exactly, but . . .) and then erase the point. He has emptied his mind. He—his seeing-point—is gazing at the luminous screen of his consciousness, but seeing no particular thing. His awareness has become like a TV screen after the station has signed off for the night. The set is still on, the screen is still aglow, but there are no pictures. When one thus gazes into undifferentiated emptiness, it is the opposite of what is usually meant by empty-headedness. It is anything but sleep. It is a totally

[2]Thankfulness: J., Kansha 感謝: literally, "feeling-gratitude."

awakened state requiring the intensest mental effort to sustain. The slightest relaxing of concentration and it will be lost: a draft on one's neck, the creak of a board, somebody's cough, and all at once everything comes tumbling back onto the screen of the consciousness again.

There are many testimonies of experiences of mind-emptying which have occurred to seekers while not engaged in Za-zen. Remember that although Kapleau had been spending many hours doing Za-zen, with Jōshū's Mu as his Kōan, the experience of emptying which he describes was not during Za-zen but during San-zen; that is, during an interview with his Rōshi: "All at once the roshi, the room, every single thing disappeared in a dazzling stream of illumination . . . . I was alone—I alone was."[3] As for myself, I have never experienced the emptied consciousness except during the practice of Za-zen.

But it does not matter when, how, or even if the emptied consciousness is experienced. The emptying is but a means to a single all-important end: to be able to go about one's ordinary occupations in the everyday world with the tranquility of realizing that everything, just as it is, is Only-Mind and, therefore, to be welcomed without hesitation or discrimination. If this realization is attained without mind-emptying, who needs mind-emptying? The whole point is learning how to cope with life in the familiar world of people, places, and things. Let me remind you again that in the Oxherding Pictures, it was after the picture of the empty circle that the climax of Enlightenment was represented. The climactic, final picture showed a man entering the marketplace of ordinary affairs with a knowing smile upon his face.

[3]Kapleau, *Three Pillars*, p. 228.

The goal of Enlightenment is not empty Emptiness, but full Emptiness!

Here is the testimony of a retired Japanese government worker—a Zen layman, not a monk—who describes his coming to Enlightenment while doing Za-zen, but moving at the moment of his Awakening from an experience of emptied mind into the ordinary world of bells, flowers, of walking about in a room, of looking at the simple objects it contained. You will note that although he is seeing familiar things, he is seeing them quite differently than before his Awakening.

He had already had a full day of doing Za-zen, but in his eagerness, he was unwilling to stop in spite of considerable discomfort:

> Centering my energy in my hara (stomach), I began to feel exhilarated. Intently I watched the still shadow of my chin and head until I lost awareness of them in a deepening concentration. As the evening wore on, the pain in my legs became so grueling that even changing from full- to half-lotus didn't lessen it. My only way of overcoming it was to pour all my energy into single-minded concentration on Mu. Even with the fiercest concentration to the point of panting "Mu! Mu! Mu!" there was nothing I could do to free myself of the excruciating pain except to shift my posture a little. Abruptly the pains disappear, there's only Mu! Each and every thing is Mu. "Oh, it's *this*!" I exclaimed, reeling in astonishment, my mind a total emptiness. "Ting-a-ling, ting-a-ling"—a bell's ringing. How cool and refreshing! It impels me to rise and move about. All is freshness and purity itself. Every single object is danc-

> ing vividly, inviting me to look. Every single thing occupies its natural place and breathes quietly. I notice zinnias in a vase on the altar, an offering to Monju, the Bodhisattva of Infinite Wisdom. They are indescribably beautiful![4]

Mu, of course, is the Japanese term I have translated as No-thing throughout the book. During the first moments of his Enlightenment he experiences the emptied Mind. He exclaims, "There is No-thing! Each and every thing is No-thing." His mind is a "total emptiness" which excludes even the agonizing pain in his legs.

But he tells us that almost immediately the world of sounds and sights returns. The same old things are there, but they are new. A bell sound is "cool and refreshing!" He finds himself rising to his feet effortlessly without any deliberate decision to do so. He is impelled "to rise and move about" in response to the ringing of the bell. Everything in the room appears to dance, to pulsate with an almost palpable newness, a curious freshness, a purity. Each thing is vividly itself, inviting attention. Each thing is sensed to be in its natural, its proper place, just as it is. He had seen the zinnias in the vase before his Awakening; now they have an entirely different quality of beauty which was previously invisible to him: they have become "indescribably beautiful!"

Here is a very lucid illustration of what I am trying to get across in this chapter: that the living experience of Enlightenment is not withdrawal from things, but going about in the ordinary world seeing the familiar from a totally new perspective. The objects you perceive do not change, but

[4]Ibid., p. 238.

there has been a complete revolution in your manner of perceiving them.

What is the nature of this revolution? It is the change from believing the things you see are outside your mind, to realizing that they are actually inside your mind. Your mind becomes Only-Mind. It is not mere intellectual assent to these words; it is an existential experience in which the fact that everything you know is an image inside your mind becomes a felt reality. (In the previous chapter I pointed out that the science of epistemology says it *is* a fact.) Even those of us who believe in the existence of an external world must admit that the only things we can actually perceive are pictures within the doorless, windowless chamber of the mind. To realize them as such is the essence of the Enlightenment experience.

In the testimony of the Japanese government worker, you have as accurate a description of how it feels to see things thus as you are apt to find. He is taken by surprise! "Oh, it's *this*!" he exclaims. The surprise is in the transformation of the familiar, or perhaps I should say, in the familiarity of the transformed. From my own personal experience, I can testify both to the accuracy and also to the inadequacy of his account of how things seem. It is as he says, but more!

I, a Jesus-man, know the Myōkō, the Mysterious-Joy, of walking the world the Zen Way. But I have chosen, and choose anew each day, to go the Jesus Way. If what I wanted was sheer, uninterrupted delight, freedom forevermore from tensions, struggles, the frustrations of failure, the aching load of responsibility, the agony of grief, the ache of guilt—if that is all I wanted, I would go Zen. Zen works, you know. It really works. Such benefits as these it does truly bring.

Why would anyone having discovered a road to this sort of paradise decide to pass it by?

I can answer for myself by saying that above any wish for tranquility and deliverance from suffering I have a hunger for truth. And, although I understand well that my conscious experience of the world could be explained logically on Zen presuppositions, I myself cannot escape the belief that in truth I am a real individual living in a world external to my mind. I am convinced that in truth I am a self-determining Ego-center with a three-dimensional body which is an integral extension of my self. I am constrained to the certainty that in truth the people I meet are other than myself and, like myself, individual Ego-centers with bodily extensions.

To believe that such things are actually true is to renounce the Zen Way. To live Zen I would have to become convinced that I am Only-Mind and not a single thing is anything but my thought. A genuine Zenist is one who has chosen to risk everything on the belief that such ideas are *true*. If the reader has absolute certainty that Only-Mind is all that *is*, then he has entered the Zen Way and can abide in its limitless tranquility, safe in the Emptiness which no form of suffering can ever penetrate.

I can induce the experience in myself by deliberately holding my critical judgment in abeyance, and can know the serenity of perfect deliverance, of utter freedom, of ultimate escape. In the vocabulary of my friends on Berkeley's Telegraph Avenue, it is a good trip, without the aid of drugs. I can induce the experience by pretending, but to go the Zen Way seriously would require me to establish my life on what would be for me a willful act of self-deception. I do not speak for anyone else. I say that for *me* a world of externally existing kittens and clouds and overalls and ovens and pineapples and people is the *truth*. Believing this, I must go forth to embrace the scratch of its brambles, the tang of its orchard scent, the weaknesses and strengths of its political systems, the Lovelessness in myself and others, the imponderable mysteries of How, the malling load of accepted responsibility—the whole ball of wax. And I choose Jesus as the key to what it is all about. I have already said as clearly as I know how what I mean by walking the Jesus-Agape-Way, the way of the cross with its Love-Pain and its promise of re-creation Jesus-ward. This too is a faith-choice, but I believe it is a faith which explains the facts of experience.

I do not choose it because I like it; I choose it because I am convinced it is *true*.

• 38 •

IN THIS final chapter I will try to draw together the concepts previously introduced and clarify the chief points of contrast between the Zen Way and the Jesus Way. Granting as obvious the universality of human nature, I readily accept the similarities of emotional and intellectual experience of people everywhere regardless of whatever religious beliefs they may hold. In this book I have sought to get behind these easily recognized similarities to consider the characteristic life-stance of the followers of Zen and the followers of Jesus which has its roots in the two faiths. My purpose has been to compare religions, not people.

A meaningful comparison requires that we examine the religions as expounded by their long trained and deeply committed adherents and as set forth in the writings sacred to these religions. Of course a comparative study of nominal Buddhism and nominal Christianity would be a valid subject for academic investigation, but it has not been the subject considered in this book.

The heart of any religion is what it requires its followers to believe, the basic presuppositions of that religion. Given those presuppositions, the valid doctrines of that religion can for the most part be found through a strict application of deductive reasoning. It has, therefore, been my purpose to uncover the premises upon which the Zen Way and the Jesus Way are established. It is as one sets those premises side by side that the mutual exclusiveness of the two faiths becomes apparent.

Here I state them once again, giving them mathematical formulation for the sake of brevity and clarity. Keep in mind the axiom that things equal to the same thing are equal to each other.

1. Presuppositions of the Zen Way:

   Only-Mind = I myself = You = the Creator = $x = y = z =$ Everything = Nothing

   (x and y and z can be anything you like; for example, Jesus, Buddha, Mohammed; the *Hannya-Shin-gyō*, the Bible, the Koran; Agape, hate, indifference; good, evil, ethical relativism; truth, error, the relativity of knowledge; Enlightenment, Ignorance, the Middle-Way; birth, life, death)
2. Presuppositions of the Jesus Way:

   (a) (character of the Creator = the ground of all valid moral laws = character of Jesus = essence of ultimate reality = character of God's Holy Spirit = character of God = Good = Agape as revealed in Jesus = character of man as intended by the Creator = character of man who has been completely re-created through giving himself to the Lordship of Jesus) ≠ (character of man who has chosen to reject the will of his creator = sin = Agapelessness = what man shall more and more become who will not repent and be reconciled to his Creator)

(b) Creator ≠ creation; I ≠ Thou; deeds of Agape ≠ deeds of Eros and Philos unsubservient to Agape; righteousness ≠ sin; subject ≠ object; the way of trust in Jesus ≠ the way of doubt in Jesus; Zen Way ≠ Jesus Way

Although the list of things equal to each other could be extended infinitely for Zen, the insertion of x, y, and z is intended to suggest some of the possibilities. The first formulation of the premises of the Jesus Way could be shortened simply to:

$$\text{(Jesus-Agape = righteousness)} \neq \text{(rejection of Jesus-Agape = sin)}.$$

After my long discussion of what lies behind the words "Jesus-Agape," the rest in the long formula—and much more—can easily be inferred. The list of nonequalities in the latter formula related to the Jesus Way could be considerably expanded, but I believe it is sufficient to suggest the ultimate incompatibility of the epistemology of Jesus and the epistemology of Zen.

Whatever else the reader may gain from this book, I hope he will forevermore be delivered from the easy sentiment of unbridled Philos which feels that all religions are roads to the same destination and that the differences between them are no more than the difference between tweedledum and tweedledee. What I am talking about here is not a diversity of vocabulary for describing the same reality; I am talking about utterly contrary conceptions of the nature of reality. Those who say all religions are essentially the same either have little substantial information on the matter, or else they are committed to a Zenlike monistic philosophy which demands the denial of all differences as a necessary dogma of their religious faith. These must preach "tolerance," with avid intolerance for anyone who disagrees.

A glance at the presuppositions of the Zen Way and the presuppositions of the Jesus Way in their mathematical formulation shows immediately where their difference lies: it lies in their diametrically opposed convictions concerning difference. Zen believes in nondifference; Jesus believes in radical difference. A mathematical statement of the Zen premise is an endless series of $=$; a mathematical statement of Jesus' premises is replete with $\neq$.

To prevent any possible misunderstanding on this point concerning nondifference and difference, I want to close with a few specific examples. With what has been given the reader in this book, he can go ahead on his own and supply many more.

ONENESS: Zen is not alone in speaking of the oneness of ultimate reality. The New Testament says the Creator is one, that Jesus is one with the Creator, and that men can become one with Jesus and through him, one with their Creator and with one another.

For Jesus-people, God the Father, God the Son, and God the Holy Spirit are not three Gods. Whatever else they may be, the Father is God in his fullness; Jesus is the perfect embodiment of God in human form; the Holy Spirit is God's power to indwell and transform any man who will let him. The Father is perfect Agape; the Son is perfect Agape; the Holy Spirit is perfect Agape. The oneness between these three is identity-oneness. Christianity is not polytheistic.

But the oneness between the Creator and his creations is harmony-oneness, not identity. Sin fractures this harmony-oneness; repentance, trust, and re-creation restore it. In this sense, a man who has entrusted himself to God is one with God. Brothers of the faith are also joined in harmony-oneness. The necessary premise of functioning Agape is a plurality of separate, self-determining selves. Christianity is not pantheistic.

I have heard Zenists including Suzuki himself say that Zen Compassion necessarily presupposes absolute identity between the "relating selves." Of course it does. Such Compassion (Mu-en-no-jihi) requires the essential No-Self-ness of the "individuals" involved. From Zen's standpoint, I-Thou-Agape is a notion rooted in Ignorance. Although—like Compassion—Agape is wholly impartial, Agape's essence is serious involvement in the needs of individuals who are genuinely other. The essence of Compassion, on the other hand, is deliverance from such forms of involvement. The belief in identity-oneness is the necessary precondition of Noninvolvement-Compassion; the belief in harmony-oneness is the necessary precondition of Involvement-Agape.

When Zen speaks of the oneness of all mankind, it means literal oneness. There are no individual selves. All men are one because all men are the thoughts of Only-Mind. Not merely men, but all beings—both animate and inanimate—are joined in the identity-oneness of Not-Two.

The Jesus-man speaks of the oneness of a particular group of people who have been brought into Agape-harmony through mutual submission to the leadership of Jesus. Zen-oneness is a solo; Jesus-oneness is a symphony orchestra composed of many different instruments brought together in voluntary obedience to a single baton. People not under the leadership of that baton are outside the oneness. It excludes those who exclude themselves. In other words, no one is coerced into harmony-oneness. It is a matter of individual choice.

FREEDOM: Both Zen and Jesus say, The truth will make you free. Zen truth is the insight gained in Enlightenment. The freedom it engenders is the liberty to accept everything just as it is with no hang-ups, no inhibitions; with thankfulness and serenity. No matter how different one set of moral rules may seem from another, Zen knows there is no difference. The Enlightened One is delivered from bondage to all rules. The Enlightened One is not bound to time or space; he knows there is no time and no space. Only-Mind is at perfect liberty to think whatever thoughts it thinks. There is nothing to hinder Only-Mind, for there is No-thing but its thoughts.

The one limiting factor for Only-Mind is its own nature. It is the character of Only-Mind to think only the thoughts it thinks, and not other thoughts which it does not think. Only-Mind is not free in the sense that it can make self-conscious decisions to think one thing instead of another. It can only think what it thinks. Out of the Stored-up-Consciousness (Alaya-vijnana), the thoughts flow onto the screen of the Six-Senses, projected from the dimensionless point of the eternal Now, the One-Thought (Ichi-nen).

Anything which appears on that screen appears with total freedom. There is no censor who will try to ban certain types of images as immoral or inappropriate. There are absolutely no prohibitions to hamper the freedom of Only-Mind. It is at perfect liberty to think whatever its Stored-up-Consciousness activates it to think. The only freedom Only-Mind does not have is freedom to miss its target. The target of Only-Mind is to think the thoughts it is thinking. Only-Mind is not free to violate its own nature. Only-Mind cannot sin. And since Only-Mind is everything, nothing can sin. The impossibility of sin in Zen is a dramatic evidence of its absolute qualitative difference from the Jesus Way.

There is a sense in which Jesus-people believe the Father-Creator is not free to sin. Sin is disobedience to the Father's will. The Father wills what he wills, and what he wills is right because he wills it. It is meaningless to say that the Father might will to disobey his own will. In Jesus, he has revealed that his nature is Agape. "God is Agape." It is unthinkable that he would ever violate his own nature.

Furthermore, Jesus-people believe that Jesus does not sin. "Jesus Christ is the same yesterday and today and forever" (Hebrews 13 : 8). Jesus is always Agape. If Jesus-Agape should in any way will to be other than Jesus-Agape, he would cease being himself. This is not possible. The essential quality of a true criterion is that it does not change. Jesus-people take the Agape-Word-Become-Flesh to be the criterion by which all deeds and all deed-doers must be measured. He is "*the* way, *the* truth, and *the* life."

The Father, the Son, and the Holy Spirit of the Father and the Son never violate their own nature. They never sin. Among created beings, only man has been given the self-conscious, creative intelligence which constitutes his capacity to violate his own nature. Man is free to miss the target of perfect obedience to the Agape will of his Creator. When measured by the criterion of Christ-like Love, it is clear man has deviated from the character originally intended by his Creator to the extent that he has become a grotesque parody of true humanity. While the Zen Way is freedom from the ability to sin, the Jesus Way is both freedom to sin and, ultimately, freedom from sinning. I remind you that the hope at the end of the Jesus Way is becoming like Jesus in perfect Agape. To reach that goal, one must travel that Way. When Jesus said, "You shall know the truth and the truth shall make you free," he referred to a category of freedom which, Jesus-people believe, is possible only to those who have first chosen to travel the Jesus Way (John 8 : 32). In other words, there is a category of freedom prior to that of which Jesus speaks in this verse.

Here is an illustration which I think will make clear the two levels of freedom which are set forth in the New Testament. When driving a car, my first freedom is to decide whether to stay on the road or to turn off it into the trackless forest on either side. If I exercise my liberty to run off the road into a wilderness of trees, bushes, stones, and mud, my freedom to travel is ended. Unless I decide to extricate my car from the mud and brush and get it back on the road again, I will have used my power of free choice to renounce my freedom to journey along that road.

If, on the other hand, I exercise my liberty and choose to drive within the limits of the width of the road, a second type of freedom is provided to me by the road itself. So long as I choose to stay on the road, I am given by that road the freedom to travel smoothly and swiftly to its destination. The freedom to go off the road is the freedom to abandon freedom, motion, and goal. The freedom *of* the road is the freedom to go where it leads.

As a Jesus-man, I believe the primary freedom of every human creature is to choose whether or not to travel the Truth-road, the Jesus Way. Off the Truth-road, freedom ends, life's wheels spin impotently: it is impossible to travel that road to its destination, perfect Jesus-likeness. Having freely made the primary decision to get on the Truth-road and to stay there, I am granted a second type of freedom which is derived from the nature of the road itself. This is the freedom of its smooth surface, its carefully banked turns, its bridges, its safety signals, and its fixed extension to the destination to which it leads. When I freely choose to travel that road, it means I freely choose to accept its limitations: I must stay within the narrow confines of its width, and I must go wherever it goes.

When Jesus says, "The truth will make you free," he refers to the freedom *of* the road. Such freedom presupposes your prior choice to renounce the freedom *off* the road. Off it you would have been liberated from the necessity of staying within its narrow confines and going where it goes. And yet, paradoxically, this liberation from the limits of the Truth-road is bondage to roadlessness. The freedom of the Jesus Way is bondage to the road.

I have already shown that along the Zen Way, the freedom to choose between truth and error is a meaningless concept. Since the condition of being on the road and off it are equally Only-Mind, both situations are equally free. In Zen the freedom *of* the road is identical to the freedom *off* it. There is total liberty; there are no limitations either way. But there is no freedom to choose deliberately to stay off the road or to go onto it. If Only-Mind is thinking *off*, it is off; if Only-Mind is thinking *on*, it is on.

This means that faithfulness to Zen delivers the Zen-man from the need to affirm the truth of Zen. If Zen is true, truth and error are Not-Two. Where Zen is, Zen is; but it is neither true nor false.

Since in Zen there is no Truth-road with its inherent limits of narrowness and fixed extension, there can be no freedom *of* the road of the type mentioned by Jesus. In Zen there is no space-extension and no time-extension, hence a serious teleology is absurd. Progress toward a goal is a violation of the presuppositions of Zen. Zen offers deliverance from interest in historical development, whether of nations or of individual persons. There are no obstacles to be overcome, no changes to be sought. Zen is freedom from striving to achieve. Zen is the freedom not to choose.

This brings into sharp focus the absolute contrast between the Zen Way and the Jesus Way. The Jesus Way is toward the fulfillment of the Creator's ultimate goals. As men yield to his will, they become both the objects and the instruments of his creative processes. Under him the history of nations and the history of individuals are progress toward his Loving aims. The Jesus Way is teleological from start to finish. Again and again Jesus speaks of the progressive growth of the Kingdom of God. The dominion of the Creator's Agape-Spirit is quietly permeating society as a pinch of yeast leavens a lump of dough. As a tiny mustard seed grows into a large plant, so the Kingdom of God began with the seed of the Son of God and is growing into a mighty plant, his universal church.

And the precondition of the spread of Agape's rule is the capacity of human creatures to select or reject the Truth-road. The French Existentialist Jean-Paul Sartre states the Christian understanding of the human situation when he writes, "Freedom is freedom to choose, but not freedom not to choose. Not to choose, in fact, is to *choose* not to choose."[1] Such an assertion rests upon the presuppositions of Materialistic Pluralism which constitute the roadbed of the Jesus Way.

Zen freedom is the freedom not to choose.

Jesus' freedom is "not freedom not to choose."

*

Toward the end of the interview with Daisetz Suzuki

[1]Quoted by Paul Foulquie, *Existentialism*, trans. Kathleen Raine (London: Dennis Dobson, 1950), p. 92.

(pp. 147–48), I said that while Buddhism accepts all things, just as they are, as good, Jesus-people find things imperfect and therefore strive to change them. To this Suzuki surprisingly replied, "Yes, that's the good side of Christianity. Buddhists accept everything as it is, perhaps. That is bad. They don't go out of their way to do good."

It is difficult for me not to believe he meant this seriously. It seemed to me that at that moment he departed from his Zen presuppositions and expressed a genuine value judgment. Whether he did, or whether he remained Only-Mind viewing himself, me, and the entire interview with complete detachment, the value judgment he articulated is crucial.

From the Zen point of view, not going out of one's way to do good is evidence of Enlightenment, as also would be not going out of one's way not to do good. Picking and choosing and the urge to "do good" are evidences of Ignorance. The freedom of the Zen Way is the freedom not to choose. But the freedom of the Jesus Way denies one the freedom not to choose. If Suzuki seriously meant what he said . . . ? Who can know? But if he *did* mean it seriously he, at least for that moment, was off the Zen Way and perilously close to the entrance of the Jesus Way.

*

It is no accident that the chief symbol of the Zen Way is a lotus blossom, and the chief symbol of the Jesus Way is a cross. No matter how filthy may be the scum on the surface of a pool in which a lotus grows, none of that scum sticks to the immaculate petals. Nothing adheres to a lotus blossom, hence it is a perfect emblem of Detachment. All things ceaselessly lap the consciousness-petals of Only-Mind, but none of them stick to it. Since everything is No-thing, Only-Mind is attached to nothing at all.

If the lotus symbolizes absolute Detachment, the cross is the symbol of total Involvement. Believing in real individual ego-centers, each with three-dimensional bodily extension, believing that each of those ego-centers has freedom of self-determination, Jesus totally involved himself in their lives. The depth of his Involvement was epitomized in his willingness to submit himself to be murdered by them. This ultimate act of Involvement, Jesus' death on the cross, revealed two things: the consequence of Agape-rejection, and the consequence of Agape-acceptance.

The consequence of Agape-rejection was the cross. Men were so deformed by Lovelessness that they could not recognize the very image of what they had been created to be. Repelled by it, they crucified Perfect-Love.

The consequence of Agape-acceptance was likewise the cross. Being wholly yielded to the Creator's Agape-Spirit, Perfect-Love accepted death at the hands of the Loveless ones for the purpose of stinging them awake to their own deformity. Their awakening to repentance with its accompanying trust-longing to be restored to the image of Jesus-Agape were precisely the conditions to make it happen. Such repentance and such trust are the acts of human free will which put men right with God. Once reconciled to him through a repentance-trust response to the cross-revelation of their own Lovelessness and God's perfect Love, men were opened to the infilling of his Agape-Spirit. By this Holy Spirit's power they would exorably be re-created into the likeness of Jesus.

Those who have been put right with God through encounter with the cross, themselves mount the same cross. Through the manifestation of Agape, the ceaseless dying to self by all who travel the Jesus Way, Jesus' own crucifixion is extended in time and space. The total Involvement of Jesus in the needs of men, as portrayed in his death, is repeated in the life of every person who comes to him. Jesus said, "If any man would come after me, let him . . . take up his cross daily and follow me" (Luke 9:23 RSV).

The cross thus pictures total Involvement in the lives of others for the purpose of their re-creation into the likeness of Jesus. The lotus blossom symbolizes the total Detachment of Zen based on its Realization that there are no others.

*

For the Zen-man, the Zen Way and the Jesus Way are Not-Two.

For the Jesus-man, the Zen Way and the Jesus Way are absolutely and irreconcilably Two.

*

BUDDHA:

One who seeks to attain Highest Enlightenment should cherish only one thought, namely, when I attain this Highest Enlightenment, I will deliver all beings. And when one has attained Highest Enlightenment, all beings are already delivered. One then knows not a single being has ever been delivered. Why? Because if an Enlightened One should believe in the existence of himself, other selves, or any beings he could not be called an Enlightened One. . . . (The Diamond Sutra)

JESUS:

I am the way, the truth, and the life; no one comes to the Father, but by me. If you had known me, you would have known my Father also; henceforth you know him and have seen him. . . . He who has seen me has seen the Father. . . . (The New Testament)

ment of Jesus in the needs of men, as portrayed in his death, is repeated in the life of every person who comes to him. Jesus said, "If any man would come after me, let him . . . take up his cross daily and follow me" (Luke 9 : 23 RSV).

The cross thus pictures total Involvement in the lives of others for the purpose of their re-creation into the likeness of Jesus. The lotus blossom symbolizes the total Detachment of Zen based on its Realization that there are no others.

*

For the Zen-man, the Zen Way and the Jesus Way are Not-Two.

For the Jesus-man, the Zen Way and the Jesus Way are absolutely and irreconcilably Two.

*

BUDDHA:

One who seeks to attain Highest Enlightenment should cherish only one thought; namely, when I attain this Highest Enlightenment, I will deliver all beings. And when one has attained Highest Enlightenment, all beings are already delivered. One then knows not a single being has ever been delivered. Why? Because if an Enlightened One should believe in the existence of himself, other selves, or any beings he could not be called an Enlightened One. (The Diamond Sutra)

JESUS:

I am the way, the truth, and the life; no one comes to the Father, but by me. If you had known me, you would have known my Father also; henceforth you know him and have seen him. . . . He who has seen me has seen the Father. (The New Testamen

GLOSSARY

AGAPE (A-ga-pe): New Testament Greek term for the distinctive type of Love manifest in Jesus and believed to be the definitive quality in the character of God. Impartial, other-centered, redemptive Love.

ALAYA-VIJNANA: *See* Stored-up-Consciousness.

ARAYA-SHIKI: *See* Stored-up-Consciousness.

AS-IS-NESS: J., Shin-nyo 眞如, literally, "true-thus-ness." Rendered by Suzuki and others as, "*Aru ga mama de yoroshii*" (Things are good just as they are). Skt., Tathata.

BIRUSHANA: Japanese transliteration of the Skt., Vairochana Buddha.

BODAI: *See* Bodhi.

BODHI: J. Bo-dai 菩提. Skt., term built on the root, Bod- or Bud-, meaning to awaken from sleep. A designation of the experience of Enlightenment.

BUDDHA: J., Butsu or Hotoke 佛. Skt., term built on the root, Bod- or Bud-, meaning to awaken from sleep. A designation for a person who has experienced Enlightenment.

BUDDHA-MIND: J., Bus-shin 佛心. A designation for Only-Mind, especially when it realizes the true nature of things.

BUDDHA-REALITY: J., Bus-shō 佛性. The real nature of things: not external objects, but thoughts of Only-Mind.

BUS-SHIN: *See* Buddha-Mind.

BUS-SHŌ: *See* Buddha-Reality.

BUTSU: *See* Buddha.

CHI-E: *See* Understanding.

CHŪ-DŌ: *See* Middle-Way.

COMPASSION: J., Ji-hi 慈悲. U-en-no———; Mu-en-no——— 有縁の———; 無縁の———. The former is the sort of compassion which is emotional involvement in the needs of others; the latter is Buddhist Compassion, free of emotional involvement.

CREATOR: A Biblical designation for ultimate reality, the ground of all being, the eternal I–AM. Progress is defined as change in the direction of his will and purpose. His essential character is revealed in Jesus. It is Agape. All anthropomorphic images—all attempts to portray him in any form—are denounced by biblical writers.

EIGHT-CONSCIOUSNESSES: J., Has-shiki 八識. In terms of function, Only-Mind has six image-producing levels: sight, hearing, smelling, tasting, touching, and thinking-feeling. The seventh level is the Spectator-Consciousness, the eighth is the Stored-up-Consciousness, q.v.

EMPTINESS: J., Kū 空. Skt., Sūnyatā. Denotes the nonobjectivity and nonsubstantiality of the sensory world.

ENLIGHTENMENT: J., Bo-dai 菩提; Satori 悟; Ken-shō 見性: Various terms which designate the experience of Awakening to the realization that Only-Mind is everything.

EROS: A Greek term for sexual love used in this book to designate all forms of bodily desire.

ETERNAL LIFE: A New Testament term for the quality of life motivated by Agape. Experienced here and now, Jesus-people believe it reaches its final perfection following the Resurrection.

FATHER: *See* Creator. The chief practical significance of the Father-son imagery in the New Testament is likeness in character, filial obedience to the Father's will, and dependence upon the Father.

FU-ICHI: *See* Not-One.

FU-NI: *See* Not-Two.

FOUR NOBLE TRUTHS: J., *Shi-shō-tai* 四正諦. Summarized in Japanese: Ku-Shū-Metsu-Dō. *Ku*: the universality of suffering; *Shū*: the cause of suffering, attachment; *Metsu*: the annihilation of suffering, the eradication of attachment; *Dō*: the Eightfold Way to eradicate attachment.

GOD: *See* Creator and Father. "God is Agape" (1 John 4 : 8).

GŌ: *See* Karma.

HAS-SHIKI: *See* Eight-Consciousnesses.

HAS-SHŌ-DŌ: *See* Noble Eightfold Path.

HEAVEN and HELL: Not spatial localities, but spiritual states. Heaven is the condition of obedience to Agape; Hell is the condition of rejecting Agape, each finally perfected following the Resurrection.

HI-SHIRYŌ: *See* No-Thought.

HI-U; HI HI-U: *See* Middle Way.

HOLY SPIRIT: The Creator's Spirit of which Jesus was begotten and of which all who become children of God are begotten. His essential character is Agape. "God's Agape is continuously poured out into our hearts through that Holy Spirit given to us" (1 Corinthians 5 : 5).

HŌ-BEN: *See* Useful Means.

HOTOKE: *See* Buddha.

ICHI-NEN; SAN-ZEN: *See* One-Thought; Three-Thousand-Realms.

IGNORANCE: J., *Mu myō* 無明; literally, "no-light." Skt., Avidya. The state of mind in which it is believed there are actual, individual selves, three-dimensional objects in three-dimensional space, linear time, subject and object, etc. Opposite of Enlightenment.

IS-SHIN. *See* One-Mind.

-JI: As a suffix to temple names it means Buddhist temple 寺. For example, Kinkaku-ji, Nanzen-ji.

JIHI: (mu-en-no———; u-en-no———): *See* Compassion.

JI-RIKI: *See* Self-Power.

JŌDO-SHIN-SHŪ: *See* True-Pure-Land-Sect.

KANNON BOSATSU: Bodhi-sattva of Compassion.

KAN-SHA: *See* Thankfulness.

KARMA: J., *Gō* 業. Skt., literally meaning "deeds"; each deed contributing to the future destiny of those caught in the wheel of rebirths, Samsara.

KEN-SHŌ: *See* Enlightenment.

KINGDOM OF GOD: A New Testament expression for the rule of Agape in human hearts. All who are subject to Agape are in his Kingdom. The final fulfillment follows the resurrection.

KŌ-AN: 公案; literally, "public edict." An anecdote from Zen history used as a focus of meditation during Za-zen.

KŪ: *See* Emptiness.

LOVE: Used capitalized in this book to denote Agape. See Agape, Eros, and Philos.

MAHA-YANA: J., Dai-jō 大乘. The two main schools of Buddhism are Mahayana and Theravada (sometimes called Hina-yana; J., Shō-jō, 小乘). In general, Mahayana is a philosophical Idealism, while Theravada is a philosophical Realism. Theravada holds to the essential difference between Samsara and Nirvana; Mahayana holds to their identity. Zen is Mahayana.

MIDDLE-WAY: J., Chū-dō 中道. In Mahayana it is the way between believing in the existence and in the nonexistence of things. Its classic statement is: Hi-u; hi hi-u; literally, NOT-

EXIST; NOT NOT-EXIST: 非有非非有. Only-Mind is everything; everything is No-thing. Hi-u; hi hi-u.

MU: *See* No-thing.

MU-GA: *See* No-thing-Self.

MU-KEI-GE: *See* No-Obstacle.

MU-MYŌ: *See* Ignorance.

MYŌKŌNIN: *See* Mysterious-Joy-People.

MYSTERIOUS-JOY-PEOPLE: J., Myōkōnin 妙好人. A designation for those who live the experience of Enlightenment in the ordinary affairs of daily life. Used especially for those who experience Thankfulness before Amida Butsu as taught in the Jōdo Shin Sect.

NAMU-AMIDA-BUTSU: 南無阿彌陀佛. The followers of Jōdo-shin-shū express Thankfulness by reciting these words orally or silently, often thousands of times each day. Literally it means something like "Hail, Amitābha Buddha."

NEHAN: *See* Nirvana.

NEM-BUTSU: 念佛; literally, "think Buddha." The practice of expressing Thankfulness to Amida through repeating, "Namu Amida Butsu."

NIRVANA: J., Ne-han 涅槃. Skt. term for the state of mind in which it is realized that Only-Mind is everything. *See* Enlightenment. Zen experiences Nirvana in Samsara; Theravada holds that they are mutually exclusive states. The word means "blown out"; it is the condition in which attachment and desire are extinguished.

NOBLE EIGHTFOLD PATH: J., Has-shō-dō 八正道. The fourth of the Four Noble Truths, q.v.

NO-OBSTACLE, NO-OBSTRUCTION, INTERPENETRATION: J., Mu-kei-ge, or Mu-ge 無罣礙. Term signifying that there are no boundaries, no shells, no skins, no insulation, no limitations to separate one thing from another. Each thing is in everything; everything is in each thing.

NOT-ONE: J., Fu-ichi. 不一. Zen says both Not-One and Not-Two.

NO-THING: J., Mu 無. In ordinary usage the word can mean simple negation: "no" or "not." In Zen it means that not a single thing exists as a three-dimensional entity in three-dimensional space. I have translated it "No-thing" to emphasize the Zen significance. Only-Mind is everything and every single thing is No-thing.

NO-THING-MIND: J., Mu-shin 無心. Only-Mind is not a thing, not a particular object in space. No-thing-Mind is One-Mind in the sense that it is Not-Two, but it is also Not-One.

NO-THING-SELF: J., Mu-ga 無我. Skt., An-atman. There are no individual selves, no I-Thou relationships. The true self is not other than Only-Mind. I am Only-Mind; Only-Mind is everything.

NO-THOUGHT: J., Hi-shiryō 非思量. Refers to spontaneous, unselfconscious action of the type engendered by Enlightenment.

NOT-TWO: J., Fu-ni 非二. There is no plurality. There are no subject and no object, no I and no you, no this and no that. And just as there are Not-Two, there is Not-One. There is not a single thing. Zen is Non-Dualism. It is also Non-Monism.

NOUMENA: Used in this book in the Kantian sense to designate things as they are in themselves beyond the mind's experience of them. This is not a Zen concept. Kant believed the Noumenal world existed outside his mind even though his knowledge of it was limited to sensory and mental responses to it. Zen says there is nothing outside the mind.

ONE-MIND: J., Is-shin 一心. The One-Mind is Only-Mind, but is No-thing-Mind. *See* No-thing-Mind and Only-Mind.

ONE-THOUGHT; THREE-THOUSAND-REALMS. J., Ichi-nen; san-zen 一念三千. The Three-Thousand-Realms represent all possible modes of being, all worlds, the whole universe. One-Thought is the timeless Now of Only-Mind's consciousness. Everything which was, is, and ever shall be exists in that One-Thought.

ONLY-MIND: J., Yui-shin 唯心. This is perhaps the most useful of all the various designations of reality as experienced by Zen. There is Only-Mind: nothing more, nothing less. No-thing exists outside Only-Mind; everything exists as Only-Mind. It is the One-Mind which is No-thing-Mind.

OTHER-POWER: J., Ta-riki 他力. Contrasted with Self-Power, the followers of Jōdo-Shin-shū trust Amida Butsu, the Other-Power, for their experience of Enlightenment instead of practicing Za-zen and other disciplines by means of Self-Power. In fact, the Self and the Other are Not-Two. A Hō-ben for inducing Thankfulness.

PHENOMENA: *See* Noumena. Phenomena is used in this book in the Kantian sense to designate the sensory and mental experiences which the mind can know directly. They are responses to the Noumenal world outside the mind; hence Phenomena is not a Zen term.

PHILOS: A Greek term signifying love for the likable, the pleasant, the congenial. It is love for family and friends. It can include abstractions among its objects: love of knowledge (philo-sophy), love of traditions, love of country, etc. As in the case of Eros, Philos is an I-Need form of love. It is partial; it takes care of its own. *See* Eros and Agape.

PLURALISTIC MATERIALISM OR MATERIALISTIC PLURALISM: I have used such expressions to designate the epistemological premise of the Christian doctrine of creation, namely, that there are many three-dimensional things in three-dimensional space. I am well aware of the ultimate identity between matter and energy on the subatomic level. On the level of human experience, however, I believe a material world measurable by Euclidean geometry exists. I believe a world outside my mind exists. Although I can only know Phenomena, I believe there is a Noumenal world of things as they are in themselves.

RECONCILIATION: When through dependent trust one yields his will to the Agape-Spirit of his Creator, this one has been reconciled to the ground of his being. The switch is closed allowing the re-creating power to flow. As this relationship is sustained, the trusting individual is remade into Jesus' image.

RESURRECTION: The New Testament does not teach that a man has a soul which leaves his body at death and lives on for eternity. Man is a psychosomatic whole. When he dies, not only his body, but also his soul (his ego) ceases to be. The New Testament faith is that there will be a resurrection at the time of Jesus' Second Coming. The consummation of the re-creation of the reconciled will occur at that time. "When he appears we shall be like him" (1 John 3 : 2). Those who have died will receive "spiritual bodies" (1 Corinthians 15 : 44).

RIN-NE: *See* Samsara.

ROKU-SHIKI: *See* Six-Senses.

SAMSARA: J., Rin-ne 輪廻; literally, "wheel-turning." Skt. term for the endless round of death and rebirth as determined by the Karma law of causation. The varying grades of existence possible throughout the whole universe of the Three Thousand Realms. Zen, and Mahayana in general, believes that Nirvana is experienced in Samsara. Another Japanese term for Samsara is Shō-ji 生死; literally, "birth-death."

SATORI: *See* Enlightenment.

SELF-POWER: J., Ji-riki 自力. In contrast to Other-Power, it is the way of attaining Enlightenment through self-discipline such as doing Za-zen, walking the Noble-Eightfold-Path, etc. From the Zen standpoint, the Self and the Other are Not-Two.

SHIN-NYO: *See* As-is-ness.

SHIN-TAI; ZOKU-TAI; *See* Truth (the Buddhist concept of Truth).

SHI-SHŌ-TAI: *See* Four Noble Truths.

SIN: The New Testament most often uses the Greek term *hamartia*, meaning that an arrow misses its target, to designate Sin. For Jesus-people, the target is to Love as Jesus loved, to be perfectly obedient to Agape. Every slightest deviation from unselfish, impartial, Jesus-like Love is Sin. Sin is disobedience to the will of God. God always wills Love.

SIX-SENSES: J., Rok-kon 六根, Roku-nyū 六入, or Roku-shiki 六識. The first means "six-roots," the second, "six-entries," the third, "six-consciousnesses." They are the usual five senses plus a sixth consisting of intellection and emotion. As Rokkon (six roots) implies, each of the six "senses" in fact is an aspect of Only-Mind which originates the aspects of consciousness associated with it.

SONS OF GOD: The New Testament says that those who are born of God's Agape-Spirit are children (or sons) of God (John 3 : 3–8). Since God is Agape, his children are those maturing unto more and more perfect Agape by the power of his Spirit. (1 John 4 : 7).

SPECTATOR-CONSCIOUSNESS: J., Mana-shiki 末那識. Mana is a transliteration of the Skt., Manas. This is the seventh level of the Eight-Consciousnesses. It is the unseen seer who views the lighted stage of the Six-Senses. It is this Mana-shiki which mistakenly believes that what it sees is outside the mind. It is on this level that the Turning-Over takes place causing a reappraisal of things, seeing them no longer as external objects, but as thought-images within Only-Mind.

STORED-UP-CONSCIOUSNESS: J., Araya-shiki 阿頼耶識. Araya is a transliteration of the Skt., Alaya. The familiar Him-alaya Mountains are, literally, the "Snow-Stored-up Mountains." This is the eighth level of the Eight-Consciousnesses. Although Only-Mind is not a thing and does not have parts, the Araya-shiki, the Alaya-vijnana, is the part of Only-Mind in which the yet unperceived images are stored. It is like the upper reel of a movie projector.

TA-RIKI: *See* Other-Power.

TEN-NE: *See* Turning-Over.

THANKFULNESS: J., Kansha 感謝. The attitude of trust in Amida as the giver of all things.

THERAVADA: J., Shō-jō 小乗; also Skt., Hina-yana. One of the two main groups of Buddhism. The other is known as Mahayana. Skt. term meaning traditionalists. Its scripture is the relatively brief Pali Canon. Its stronghold is such South Asian countries as Ceylon. It advocates the achievement of Enlightenment through self-discipline. It sees Nirvana as deliverance from Samsara. It is called Hina-yana (small-wagon) by Mahayanists because only a few can achieve Bodhi through its difficult way. Understandably, Theravada does not approve of this designation.

TRUE-PURE-LAND-SECT: J., Jō-do-shin-shū 浄土眞宗. That school of Japanese Buddhism which was founded by Shinran and makes use of the three chief Pure-Land sutras, the *San-bu-kyō*. It teaches birth in Amida Butsu's Pure Land to all who trust in him. The Nem-butsu is a way of expressing Thankfulness.

TRUTH AS UNDERSTOOD IN MAHAYANA: Zoku-tai 俗諦; Shin-tai 眞諦. Zoku-tai is the way of understanding characterized by Ignorance. It is belief in a true distinction between subject and object, in the existence of a world outside one's mind. Zoku means literally what is common or ordinary or vulgar; tai means "truth." Shin-tai, on the other hand, is belief in a true identity between subject and object. Shin-tai is true Understanding gained in Enlightenment that there is No-thing outside Only-Mind. Shin means "true"; Shin-tai means "true-truth." "Tai" or "tei" is not easy to translate. The term can mean resignation or reconciliation. In the word Tei-kan it means "clear-vision," in Tei-nen, "a heart that understands *truth.*" If the concepts represented by Shin-tai are true, no concepts can be considered true in any absolute or definitive sense.

TURNING-OVER: J., Ten-ne 轉依. A term to designate the revolution of viewpoint on the seventh level of the Eight-Consciousnesses of Only-Mind. When this Spectator-Consciousness suddenly realizes that the objects on the lighted stage of the Six-Senses are not outside the Mind as first supposed, this is Ten-ne.

UNDERSTANDING: J., Chi-e 智慧; Skt., Prajna. This has often been translated Wisdom. The ordinary connotation of Wisdom is skill in dealing with practical problems. Chi-e, Prajna, Jnana, and such terms refer to the insights gained in Enlightenment. There is a new Understanding of the nature of things: Only-

Mind is everything; everything is No-thing. Chi-e is not different from Shin-tai. *See* Truth.

USEFUL-MEANS: J., Hō-ben 方便; Skt., Upaya. The use of mythological images and parables to point the Mind toward Enlightenment.

YUI-SHIN: *See* Only-Mind. Sometimes also Yui-ga 唯我, meaning "only-self." The Ultimate Self is Only-Mind.

ZA-ZEN: 坐禪; literally, "seated-meditation." The primary discipline practiced in Zen temples. It is generally done in company with others in a Meditation-Hall (Zen-dō), but also can be done alone in one's own home. *See* Zen.

ZEN: 禪; Skt., Dhyana or Jhana. Usually translated Meditation, but it is not thinking about something. It is a determined attempt to empty the consciousness until one becomes conscious of consciousness alone. Often a Kōan is used as an aid to this end. Zen (Zen-shū) is also used as the name of the particular sect of Buddhism discussed in this book.

INDEX